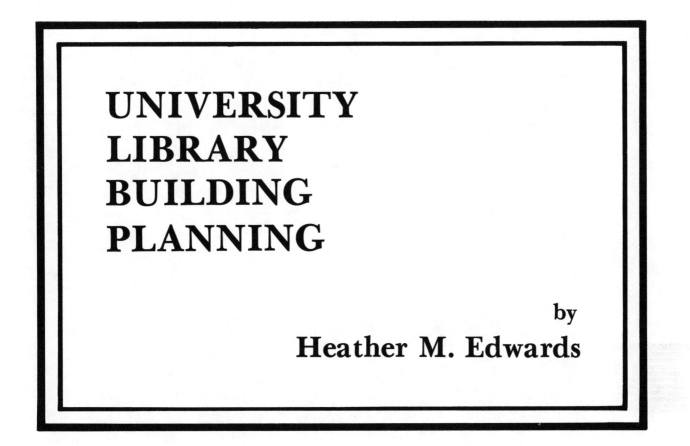

UNIVERSITY LIBRARY BUILDING PLANNING

by

Heather M. Edwards

The Scarecrow Press, Inc.
Metuchen, N.J., & London
1990

British Library Cataloguing-in-Publication data available

Library of Congress Cataloging-in-Publication Data

Edwards, Heather M., 1947–
    University library building planning.

    1. Library planning. 2. Library buildings.
3. Libraries, University and college. I. Title.
Z679.5.E37   1990   022′.317   89-24261
ISBN 0-8108-2225-3

Printed on acid-free paper

Contents

Acknowledgments

I should like to acknowledge with gratitude the encouragement and advice given to me by Reuben Musiker, Librarian at the University of the Witwatersrand, Johannesburg. I also wish to thank Godfrey Thompson for giving up time for me on the occasions I visited London, for arranging visits to numerous libraries in Britain, and for sharing with me much of his knowledge and enthusiasm for library planning and design; and Ralph Ellsworth, who gave me valuable advice on libraries to visit in North America and was a gracious host during my stay in Colorado. It has been a privilege to meet two such distinguished authors and consultants in the field of library planning, and to come to know them as friends.

I am grateful to the many librarians, too numerous to mention, who made me welcome and spent time with me when I visited their institutions; one learns a lot from such contact. I wish to acknowledge the following people in particular:

Morris Schertz, Librarian, University of Denver, from whose excellent *Building Program* I have quoted extensively; Donald O. Rodd, retired Librarian, University of Northern Iowa, and experienced planning consultant; Peter Hoare, Librarian, Nottingham University Library, who made available to me several photographs of his library; Brenda Moon, Librarian, Edinburgh University; Hennie Viljoen, Director of Library Services, University of Stellenbosch; and Henk de Bruin, Director of Library Services at the University of the Orange Free State at the time I visited this library, who also helped me with photographs.

In addition I must thank a number of publishers who have granted me permission to reproduce floor plans and diagrams, and authors whom I have quoted. They have been acknowledged at relevant points in the text.

This book is based on "University Library Planning: A Comparative Study," a dissertation submitted to the Faculty of Arts, University of the Witwatersrand, Johannesburg, 1985, in fulfillment of the requirements for the degree of Master of Arts.

Finally, and on a more personal note, I wish to thank my friend Ian Crowther, whose unwavering support, patience, and encouragement during the preparation of this book have meant a great deal to me.

Heather M. Edwards
The Library
University of the Witwatersrand
South Africa

Preface

Libraries need to work well. For most students the average academic library is a complex set of systems that does more to confuse than to help the user. A badly designed library increases people's perplexity, wastes their time, and is better avoided.

I have seen many badly designed libraries during my career as a librarian—in fact I work in one! I have also seen many excellent libraries, and it is the difference between the two that caused me to consider writing a book on university library planning. The fact that with guidance and foresight a librarian could have an attractive, functional, popular library instead of a white elephant reinforced my decision.

This book brings together basic principles of function and design and those aspects of library planning I have found to be particularly important in the building of a successful library. In the course of building projects on which I have consulted as well as new libraries for which I have been directly responsible, aspects such as space standards, advent of the new technology, audiovisual requirements, and good space management have been important considerations. This book deals with these practical considerations and will, I hope, provide librarians involved in planning with a useful checklist. On a more idealistic level, I hope that the case studies I have included will provide a general background of what works, what users enjoy, and what academic library planners should strive for.

University Library Building Planning is intended for librarians, university planners, and administrators, those on project committees, architects, and students of librarianship. A large amount of effort, financial resources, and time go into the planning of library buildings. Let us try to build attractive, functional, adaptable, congenial buildings. They are an important part of educational success and personal growth.

1 Introduction

Prior to the latter half of this century in many countries of the Western world, libraries were built on university campuses without much involvement on the part of librarians. They were provided with a building which it was hoped would last for many years, and in most cases, although with some drawbacks and inconveniences, it did. During these years librarians saw their job as one of collecting and storing printed material, providing adequate housing for these items, and of supplying users with the information they required. Librarianship was on the whole fairly conservative and innovations were viewed with suspicion.

This approach sufficed for many years while universities remained small and the volume of knowledge manageable. However, a number of factors have contributed to a dramatic change in libraries and in the general attitude of librarians, and the most important of these is probably what has been termed the "information explosion."[1] Today more information is being generated than ever before, and it is impossible for a library to contain all the information its users are likely to need. This situation will certainly escalate. As numbers of publications and their cost increase, the collections of most university libraries will in all probability become less adequate in terms of research needs, and libraries will turn to other methods of supplying information. Two facts emerge from this situation:

1. If librarians are to retain the prestige and respect they deserve within the context of the university, they are going to have to provide sufficient information to users as quickly as possible.
2. To do this, they are going to have to make extensive use of available technology. The library of today and of the future, if it is to be cost-effective and efficient, is going to have to install up-to-date telecommunication systems and computers to gather scholarly information, organize it, store it, and deliver it to users. Failure to automate will in the long term lead to obsolescence.

Branscomb[2] states:

> In our present 20th Century world of print and paper, we tend to think of information in terms of documents. In the future our information machines will permit us to enjoy more immediate access to all kinds of information-gathering capabilities. Documents will become only occasional by-products of information access, not the primary embodiment of it.

Technological developments are taking place with great rapidity, and they have already had a profound effect on libraries. Even if one does not believe that books and traditional libraries will shortly be obsolescent, maybe one should give consideration to the fact that books are a somewhat laborious way of transmitting knowledge, that to serve thousands of students many multiple copies are needed, and that the weight of books is reflected in higher architectural costs. These are the views of Cornberg, who has been called "perhaps the most radical prophet of the new library technology."[3] There are areas where modern information retrieval techniques may be used to good advantage—not in the provision of basic bookstock for undergraduate students, of manuscripts and rare books for scholars, nor of items for recreation and leisure, but in the rapid supply of scientific, bibliographical, research, statistical, and other factual data. In meeting this challenge, librarians will have to make available new and enhanced services.

The expectations of library users have changed during the last decade, and this is apparent in all aspects of library service. Problem-oriented research across many disciplines is becoming commonplace. Many users, lacking the time and background to search several indexes and abstracting journals in different fields, are relying more on librarians as intermediaries to access and evaluate the literature. In addition, as methods of education change, so too do the library needs of both teachers and students. The university of today makes use of the new technology as a means of increasing the efficiency of the learning process. The library, in support of the teaching program, must adapt to new methods, provide relevant facilities, equipment, and materials, and should take the lead in encouraging innovative methods of teaching and learning.

All aspects of the new technology will have an effect on library planning and design requirements to a greater or lesser degree. As services adapt to meet new demands, so must the buildings that house them. Library planners need to take a fresh look at the organization of space, storage of information, and access to it no matter what its format, changing user needs, or new services, and resulting from all this, the structural, mechanical, and electrical changes required to accommodate a modern library service.[4]

Also contributing to change in library design is the rapid rise in construction, material, and labor costs. Whereas in the early part of this century columned façades, lofty entrance halls, high-ceilinged reading rooms, and ornate staircases were typical features, modern libraries are the result of a reaction against some of the extravagances of pre–World War I styles. Librarians, university planners, and architects alike realized the importance of making maximum use of available funding, and the value of far-sighted planning in the form of internal flexibility and provision for expansion. The changes that took place may be summarized in the words of Macdonald:[5] "The best libraries are now built

primarily to serve readers rather than to impress them." There are numerous undeniable advantages to this approach. However, despite greater simplicity, rising costs mean that it becomes increasingly difficult to build a comfortable and functional facility that can house the wide range of materials and services required of a library today.

In the United States new academic libraries may currently cost over $200 per square foot, with most costing in the region of $100 (1987)—(±$2,000 and $1,000 per square meter respectively). Merely a few years ago, the average figure was $50 per square foot (1980)—($535 per square meter). In South Africa, where for many years building construction was relatively inexpensive, costs have risen sharply and new buildings can cost up to R650 per square meter to construct. This figure rises to over R1,000 per square meter when fittings, air conditioning, and fire protection are included.[6]

Although libraries have of necessity become more practical, they should not necessarily be functional to the exclusion of all else. Although very few librarians regret the passing of monumentality, the library should remain a symbol on a university campus, signifying its importance in academic achievement. It should be efficient and comfortable within, yet finally it is more than bricks and mortar; it is an instrument of education. Beauty and practicality are not incompatible. On the contrary, they are frequently combined with a large measure of success, and it is this combination that library planners and architects should try to achieve.

Planning a library building of any size is a highly complex exercise. Most newcomers to the process work "by the book" according to established norms and procedures, incorporating areas and spaces recommended and listed by well-respected library planners as essential in any library. Although often perfectly adequate, there is more to planning than theory. Those involved in the process need to have within them a sensitive understanding of buildings, the planning and building process, and what makes some buildings highly successful additions to society and others monumental disasters. This sensitivity is developed over years of involvement in the planning process, and through an ability to observe buildings critically and thoroughly as regards their good and bad features. Library planning is a practical rather than an abstract exercise, demanding commitment, insight, and empathy on the part of the planner or planning team.

Much may be learned about libraries through careful study of several existing buildings. For this reason I have included case studies of libraries in three countries—the United States, Great Britain, and South Africa. Such observation is especially relevant several years after completion. In the first years of a building's life, there is a sense of pride and achievement among those involved in its conception; a tendency to make excuses for areas that are not functioning quite as well as they should. It is only later that planners, feeling less vulnerable, will admit freely to mistakes made, and pinpoint areas of possible improvement. Talking to library administrators, and even more so, to the staff working in a building, can be a highly educational and beneficial exercise.

It is my intention that this book should provide library administrators with some background to and understanding of new developments in library planning. It deals with situations arising out of today's problems and tomorrow's developments—the new technology, changing methods of teaching and learning, the quantitative explosion in the amount of information available, and the qualitative explosion in the type of materials used. These developments must be reflected in the design of tomorrow's library. They require that planners account for computer installations, audiovisual centers, adequate and flexible wiring, and a new approach to the management of space. How will tomorrow's librarians deal with enormous quantities of information, miles of computer printout, and a wide variety of electronic equipment, remembering at all times that their most important function is to anticipate the needs of their patrons?[7] This book addresses these problems and answers these questions. In addition, recommendations are made to assist library planners in avoiding obsolescence—"Divine, si tu peux, et choisis, si tu l'oses" (Corneille—"Guess if you can, and choose if you dare").

REFERENCES

1. R.W. Boss, *The Library Manager's Guide to Automation* (White Plains, N.Y.: Knowledge Industry Publications, 1979), p.1.
2. L.M. Branscomb, "The ultimate frontier," in C.C. Rochell (ed.), *An information agenda for the 1980's* (Chicago: ALA, 1981).
3. A.D. Osborn, "The influence of automation on the design of a university library," in A. Kent (ed.), *Library Planning for Automation* (Washington, D.C.: Spartan Books, 1965), p.55.
4. M. Beckman, "Library buildings in the network environment," *Journal of Academic Librarianship*, vol.9, no.5, 1983, p.281.
5. A.S. MacDonald, "Looking backward and forward in library planning," *South African Libraries*, vol.21, 1953, p.3.
6. Personal communication with D. Whyte of Pearse, Aneck Hahn, Donaldson, and Whyte, architects. Johannesburg, 1987.
7. E. Cohen and A. Cohen, *Automation, Space Management, and Productivity* (New York: Bowker, 1981), p.i.

2 Desirable Qualities in Academic Library Buildings

The financial limitations imposed on library expansion in a number of countries since the mid-1970s has meant that in recent years more care has had to be taken in designing buildings that are functional, economical, and less grandiose than in the past. Concepts such as *open plan* and *flexibility* are today major considerations in most architects' design work, and *economy* both in terms of initial cost and ongoing maintenance is a control factor that greatly influences the final result. Librarians and architects work within strict budgets, and the buildings they plan must function efficiently in the broadest sense of the word.

The marked effect on library planning of a number of factors such as technological developments, changing expectations of library users, and rising costs has already been mentioned. In addition, the holdings of the various disciplines are constantly changing in relation to one another, as is the didactical picture, and the nature of the library itself is in the process of constant evolution. Although the future is difficult to predict, it is certain that greater use of available technology will have an effect on library design. Thompson[1] states: "A new library must be designed to operate with the materials and techniques of the future rather than the past." Thus a high degree of adaptability is necessary.

Despite differing internal arrangements and library services, recent successful libraries of all sizes have a number of factors in common that have been recognized by Faulkner-Brown, a leading British architect of academic libraries. These desirable qualities have become popularly known as "Faulkner-Brown's *Ten Command-*

ments,"[2] and each should be carefully considered during the initial stages of planning. A library should be:

1. **Flexible,** with a layout, structure and services which are easily adapted to changing circumstances.
2. **Compact,** for ease of movement of readers, staff and books through the building.
3. **Accessible,** from the exterior into the building and from the entrance to all parts of the building, with an easy, comprehensible plan needing minimum supplementary directions.
4. **Extendible,** to permit future growth with minimum disruption to services.
5. **Varied,** in its provision of accommodation and services to satisfy the differing needs of users.
6. **Organised,** to facilitate appropriate exposure of books and other sources of information to users.
7. **Comfortable,** to promote efficiency of use.
8. **Constant in environment,** for the preservation of library materials.
9. **Secure,** to control user behavior and loss of library materials.
10. **Economic,** to be built and maintained with minimum resources both in finances and staff.

FLEXIBILITY

A flexible library building is one in which as large an area as possible may be used for any of the library's main functions—reader space, staff space, and stack space. Metcalf[3] outlines the requirements of a flexible library as the provision of suitable heating, ventilation, and lighting in all areas in order to facilitate change; floors should be designed to carry a live load of at least 150 lbs/ft² (750 kg/m²); ceiling heights should be adequate throughout (at least 8′4″); and all parts of the library should be easily accessible. Supporting columns should be placed at regular intervals, and the number of permanent walls within the building should be kept to a minimum, preferably confined to certain core areas containing ducts, toilets, stairs, and lifts. All other walls should be demountable. For the most part the building should be open plan. Privacy may be achieved by careful placing of furniture and shelving and with the use of acoustic material on floors and ceilings. If this is done, changes may easily be made without having to undertake expensive structural alterations. In addition, the open plan library can be economical in staff resources, as informal control may be facilitated visually over large areas. At times of staff shortage it is possible for a staff member to supervise more than one department if they are informally arranged in relation to each other.[4]

However, as Thompson[5] points out, flexibility is both limiting and expensive. In return for the obvious benefits of the open plan layout, architects must provide an ideal environment in all parts of the building at greatly increased cost, and they will also find themselves restricted in their choice of design solutions. Features such as atriums, courtyards, and skylights will limit flexibility.

On a more human level, flexibility in the hands of less imaginative architects can result in featureless areas that disregard human scale and library functions. Lushington[6] believes that flexibility has become the greatest cliché in library design, and that those who rush to achieve it may be deliberately avoiding the more difficult task of providing good functional design. If every space in the library must be useful for every purpose, it is fruitless to seek special building solutions for specific needs. Various functional environments have differing characteristics that should be designed into the spaces from the outset. Only then will the user receive the best service, the student work efficiently, and the building be cost-effective.

Lushington's view is not necessarily in conflict with that of Faulkner-Brown. Spaces may be designed for specific purposes yet retain flexibility. The successful use of flexible space for the many different functions existing in a library is the challenge facing the architect and the planning team, and is a measure of their ability.

COMPACTNESS

The most compact form of building is a cube. A cube is essentially the result of modular design, wherein the floor area is made up of equal squares (or rectangles), the structure is simple, and the whole relates very well to library functional requirements. Travel distances are reduced to a minimum, on entry users are brought to the center of gravity of the building, and books, staff, and readers will move shorter distances. There is also an economy in the consumption of energy.[7]

ACCESSIBILITY

Ease of access to a building and its contents is an important factor. The approach should be logical, convenient, and attractive, and this is best achieved by locating the building in a central position, thus ensuring that journeys to the library from different parts of the campus are as short as possible. The location must be carefully considered in relation to main circulation routes and to the siting of both present and future buildings on the campus. On entering the building, the user should immediately be aware of the main elements, e.g. information desk, catalogues, and stairs. This should be achieved through design and not an overproliferation of signs.[8]

EXTENDIBILITY

The principle of the self-renewing library, whereby careful weeding of the stock takes place at the same rate as the acquisition of new stock, thereby maintaining the library's size at a predetermined level, has limited the size of academic libraries in Britain. In general, however, academic libraries worldwide are built with provision for future expansion. This may take place vertically (upward or downward) or laterally. Not all are ideal. Thompson[9] points out that upward expansion is likely to cause severe disruption to existing services. The library is perhaps the most sensitive of all educational buildings to the disturbances caused by building operations above an existing building which has to remain in use during the construction period. He also mentions that upward extension requires a heavier and thus more expensive basic structure, and special care in the placing of core elements. Lateral expansion appears to be the most suitable. Architects may very easily make use of either demountable partitions for an external wall, or precast panels which may be demounted and reused on the outer façade of the extended building.[10] Outline plans for future extensions and their relationships to the original building plan should be determined at the time the original brief is prepared, and should be used subsequently when the extension takes place. At each stage of development the building should be a complete entity.

VARIETY

Users of libraries have many different preferences regarding their surroundings. Some are gregarious, others prefer privacy; some like a view, while others require no visual disturbance at all. As much variety of seating accommodation as possible should be provided. Not only does this satisfy user needs, but it adds color and interest to the interior of the library. It is not only the building staff itself, but good furniture design and layout which are necessary for the success of the library in establishing a satisfactory relationship between user and information.

ORGANIZATION

A library should be organized in such a way that its services and stock are accessible and easily

available.[11] Simplicity of layout is vitally important, and planning should be such that there is minimum interference with the main routes through the building of both readers and material.

COMFORT

The internal environment should be carefully considered. Faulkner-Brown[12] states: "A fresh, constant temperature and humidity not only promotes efficiency of use, it encourages it." It is also necessary to provide a good level of lighting, both at the work surface and among the bookstacks. (It is generally agreed among illumination engineers that approximately 70 foot candles is the intensity of illumination desirable in libraries.) Daylight is always an advantage, especially from a psychological point of view, and for this reason reader spaces are often planned around the periphery of the building. It is however important that daylight—especially sunlight—should be carefully controlled to avoid glare and heat build-up. General illumination may have to be supplemented by local lighting in some areas, e.g. carrels and typewriting rooms, where concentrated lighting is needed. Metcalf[13] mentions that the quality of reader accommodation keeps rising, and more comfortable and convenient study conditions are required. It is unwise to attempt to economize in this area.

The interior of the library must be so designed as to smoothly, comfortably, and attractively serve the needs of its users. It is not enough that a library be functional; it is potentially the most civilizing influence on the campus if properly used, and its decor and appointments should be a clear reflection of this.[14]

In using an academic library, large numbers of patrons will inevitably create noise. Measures should be taken to reduce noise as far as possible, both in terms of design and layout of the library, and in the use of internal finishes. Soft floor coverings and acoustic treatment on ceilings combine with bookstacks and furniture to create an environment in which sound levels may be held within acceptable limits by comparatively simple means. Where normal operational sound needs to be masked, electronically generated "white sound" may be used to create an even balance in the larger spaces. Areas that naturally generate noise, such as the circulation and inquiry counters, catalogues, and reference section, should be separated from quiet study areas.

CONSTANT IN ENVIRONMENT

This factor relates closely to that of comfort. In addition to providing a suitable environment for patrons, levels of illumination, temperature, and humidity should be carefully monitored to preserve library materials. In general, a temperature of ±68°F (20°C) and a relative humidity level of 50% are considered suitable for this purpose.

SECURITY

It is important that the architect be thoroughly aware of the need for security in a library when designing its layout. There should be one public entrance/exit; the staff or delivery entrance should be fitted with a card access system or similar device; windows must be lockable, if indeed opening windows are provided; electronic security at the exit will help to reduce book loses; and fire escapes will need careful attention in order that they serve their purpose yet do not provide alternative exits from the building. An aspect of security frequently overlooked is that of staff supervision over user behavior, facilitated by open planning and careful location of service counters and staff stations.

ECONOMY

Libraries that require long hours of illumination and air conditioning are expensive buildings to run. Faulkner-Brown[15] suggests that attention be given to certain economies such as:

• Reducing the area of the external walls and roof so that the ratio of wall area to floor area

is low. Kaser[16] concurs with this, recommending rectangular buildings that can be entered near the center of the long side, especially at the middle level, as being most suited to economical library use and operation. When irregular shapes are used, much of this economy is lost. Round buildings are inefficient in their use of floor space, curves are more expensive to construct than straight lines and right angles, and most items of standard library furniture and equipment are rectangular. So are the books! Other building forms such as triangles, octagons, and parallelograms have been used by architects with varying degrees of success (Kaser), but the "box," as the standard modular library has been termed, is still the most successful and economical shape.

• Windows, which allow heat to pass easily in and out of a building, should not exceed 25% of the total wall area. Greater use of glass will result in energy inefficiency. Fenestration in a library building should be based on the needs of library users rather than the architect's wish to create some external design feature.

Most energy is required in hot weather when the air conditioning unit has to counteract high outside temperatures, and when the library is being used by large numbers of readers. As Thompson[17] points out, there are two cost factors involved—initial and running. Initial costs are predictable and small compared to running costs which depend on many uncontrollable factors, and which occur throughout the life of the building. Careful attention should be given to mechanical services and the incorporation of maintenance-free surfaces in the building. A brick or concrete wall will cost far less in upkeep than one that is plastered and painted. The initial expense of heavy-duty carpeting in areas of dense traffic will prove worthwhile and require replacing less often.

The advantages of incorporating Faulkner-Brown's *Ten Commandments* in academic library planning need little justification. There are sufficient fine library buildings in existence based on these principles to prove their relevance and value in modern library planning (e.g. Nottingham University Library, St. Andrews University Library, and Loughborough University of Technology Library in the United Kingdom). In chapters 4, 5, and 6 I have reviewed a selection of modern library buildings in the United Kingdom, the United States, and South Africa, primarily with regard to Faulkner-Brown's philosophy. Some of these libraries are very successful and achieve a rare excellence; others fall a little short of this exalted level. But all are fine examples of careful library planning.

References

1. G. Thompson, *Planning and Design of Library Buildings,* 2nd. ed. (London: Architectural Press, 1977), p.14.
2. H. Faulkner-Brown, "The open plan and flexibility," *International Association of Technological University Libraries,* Proceedings, vol.11, 1979, p.3.
3. K.D. Metcalf, *Planning Academic and Research Library Buildings* (New York: McGraw Hill, 1965), p.8.
4. Faulkner-Brown, pp.4–5.
5. Thompson, pp.36–37.
6. N. Lushington, "Some random notes on functional design," *American Libraries,* February 1976, p.92.
7. Faulkner-Brown, p.5.
8. Ibid., p.6.
9. Thompson, p.36.
10. Faulkner-Brown, p.6.
11. Ibid., p.7.
12. Ibid.
13. Metcalf, p.10.
14. P.H. Connell, "Physical planning of technikon libraries," in *The Technikon Library: A New Challenge* (Pretoria: Department of National Education, Library Services Branch, 1980), p.70.
15. Faulkner-Brown, p.8.
16. D. Kaser, "Twenty-five years of academic library building planning," *College and Research Libraries,* July 1984, p.271.
17. Thompson, p.41.

3 *University Library Space Standards*

Although buildings do not represent the most important resource of a university, they play an important role in achieving the purposes of higher education. Good planning and management of this resource is of significant value because:

- Buildings house the educational and research programs of universities, and the amount of space available may define the activities to which the institution may commit itself.
- Physical facilities consume most of the university's capital expenditure and a significant portion of its operating expenditure.
- Acquisition of buildings represents a major commitment of financial resources.
- Buildings are a highly visible resource and may strongly influence an institution's image.[1]

Managing space is primarily a case of determining how well the existing facility is functioning and estimating present and future space needs. This analysis is assisted by space standards (or norms) which serve as a starting point for assessment.[2]

Library building standards may be broadly defined as quantitative and qualitative norms that state the basic minimum physical requirements for effective library service. Although social, economic, and geographic conditions as well as existing stages of library development vary greatly, it has been found that certain fundamental requirements may be applied relatively easily to a variety of local circumstances.[3] Standards should be viewed as guidelines only, and not as rigid prescriptions. Naturally, librarians will have to decide for themselves to what extent these guidelines suit their particular needs and circumstances.

Standards do, however, form a very useful basis for library building planning; they enable a librarian to evaluate existing facilities, to quantify future needs, to answer the question, "What are the functions of my library?" As Havard-Williams[4] so rightly states:

> There is no more searching test of a librarian's competence nor of his whole conception of what a library should be, what services it should offer, and what place it should hold in the university, than the evidence shown in a building he has planned.

Although *building* standards will include consideration of aspects such as site, accessibility, relation to other facilities, and flexibility, in this chapter I am concerned primarily with *space* standards. The three norms that form the basis of all library space planning are reader stations (study), library staff (office and processing), and book storage (stack).

LIBRARY SPACE STANDARDS IN THE UNITED KINGDOM

British universities are financed and administered by the University Grants Committee (UGC). In 1963 a subcommittee under the chairmanship of Parry was established "to consider the most effective and economical arrangements for meeting the needs of universities . . . for books and periodicals."[5] However, the resulting *Parry Report* (1967) did not cover space standards comprehensively enough, and a working party was subsequently established by the UGC to make recommendations in this area. These were set out in the UGC's *Planning Norms for University Buildings (1974)*,[6] and in brief were as follows:

• Book storage was to be provided on the following scale:

	Books m²/1,000 vols.	Bound Journals m²/1,000 vols.
Open access:	4.65	9.35
Closed access (fixed):	4.03	8.06
Closed access (rolling):	2.07	4.13

With a typical mix of material this suggested some 5.83 m² per 1,000 volumes overall (62.75 ft² per 1,000 volumes).

• Reader places were to be provided at a ratio of 1 : 5 for all arts students and 1 : 7 for all science students. Provision for academic staff and postgraduate students was included in these norms, with certain exceptions.

• Administration and all other support facilities should be provided within an area of 18% of the sum of reading and book storage areas.

When a new library or major extension was planned, the UGC was prepared to take into account reasonable requirements for future growth to provide for ten years' increase in publications and student numbers. The UGC's policy at the time was thus to encourage libraries to develop their stock and services, to provide up-to-date information as well as access to older stock, and to provide suitable space and conditions in which readers could work. However, within a short space of time, the UGC was forced to reconsider these norms. The "information explosion" was causing an increase in the need for more library space, and in addition, the cost of building new libraries and extensions was rising steadily.

THE ATKINSON REPORT

A working party under the chairmanship of Atkinson was established to review the committee's policy for the provision of library buildings. The results of these investigations were published in 1976 and have become commonly known as *The Atkinson Report*. The recommendations made form the basis for university library planning in the United Kingdom.

It was intended that the policy should be realistic in its claims on resources, but should still enable universities to maintain and in some respects improve their library services.[7] As a starting point the working group endorsed the principle that reader stations should be related to planned student numbers, but it questioned the concept of providing space for the whole of a library's existing stock and proposed future acquisitions. It was felt that this would lead to indefinite accumulation which could result in organizational problems and a lessening of the efficiency of the library's service. The cost of maintaining access to the collection could well encroach upon the funds for acquisitions. The working group thus suggested the concept of the "self renewing" library in which new accessions would be balanced by the withdrawal of obsolete or unused material to other stores.

In attempting to work out academic library requirements, Atkinson's committee considered several factors, described in the report:[8]

1. *Reasonable minimum provision of shelving (excluding special collections) for the self-renewing library.* Basic to this was "whether it was reasonable to relate size of library to number of students, disregarding the length of time over which the library had been in operation." Research was carried out at universities in the United Kingdom and it was concluded that the age of a university library was not closely connected with the amount of shelving required, but that the number of full-time equivalent (FTE) students was. Results ranged from 6.59 to 2.26 m per FTE student, with the average being 3.7 m per FTE student (12.14 ft). The conclusion of the working group was that 3.8 m (12.47 ft) of shelving per FTE student would be a reasonable yardstick on which to base academic library development. Universities with departmental libraries were expected to provide for them within this allowance.

2. *Provision for future growth.* The underlying principle is that if a library is adequate at present, it will continue to be adequate if its growth at a certain rate of accessions per year is balanced by a similar rate of withdrawals. However, the volume and rate of growth of

material published is also relevant. In 1975 the working group found that the world production of monographs had been increasing at an average rate of 6% per year. There were, however, marked fluctuations, and growth appeared to be slowing down. The rate for periodicals was approximately 4%, and this too appeared to be decreasing. The committee decided that an annual growth rate of 4% in world production would be a reasonable assumption. It was then discovered that library accessions were not growing at the same rate, but in fact were fairly constant at 5.75 volumes per FTE student annually. After considering various factors, the committee concluded that an addition to the norm of 0.2 m^2 (2.15 ft^2) per FTE student should be sufficient to provide for growth in accessions over a 10-year period.

3. *Interlibrary lending, local library cooperation, and financing.* With a general reduction in acquisitions for financial reasons, one could expect an increase in the use of interlibrary lending, controlled somewhat by the increasing cost of borrowing. It is unlikely that this factor will have any effect on the space needs of libraries. Regarding local library cooperation, studies in Britain have shown that there is not much overlap among libraries. Thus little saving in space may be expected either from the disposal of existing duplicate stock or from the avoidance of duplication in new acquisitions. The financing of British universities in the future will certainly have an effect on the number of publications purchased annually, but this cannot be accurately assessed. The factors mentioned above were considered relatively unimportant in the overall calculation of space.

4. *Special Collections.* Most university libraries have special collections of books and manuscripts, often accepted under terms or conditions that preclude them from being relegated to store. In addition, they are often valuable and of scholastic importance. The working group recommended that the UGC should be prepared to consider each case separately, and to allow up to 100% of the space needed as additional to that calculated for the remainder of the bookstock. It suggested, however, that the acceptance of a donation could use a significant proportion of a university's capital, particularly where there was an obligation to keep a collection up-to-date. The committee believed that the UGC should be consulted when a university proposed to accept a collection of more than 5,000 items, so that the long-term financial consequences could be fully considered.

5. *Relegation.* Basic to this is the assumption that it is economic to withdraw annually from the stock a proportion of little-used material that will balance the current year's acquisitions. Withdrawal is a complicated and costly procedure. An interim local store should be provided, to which books may be removed and retrieved within 24 hours if required. Material still unused after five years could then be removed to a national store. Fewer problems are encountered with journals; selection is simpler and the cost of withdrawal is less in relation to the space freed. Items withdrawn *must* be stored more cheaply than in the main library.

6. *Reserve storage.* There are a number of ways in which this may be provided:

   • within an existing building or extension;
   • in a local store exclusive to the university;
   • in a local store shared with other local institutions;
   • in a regional store;
   • in a national store.

   The most practical solution is thought to be a combination of some form of local storage and a national store.

7. *Reader stations.* The existing UGC norm provided one reader station at 2.39 m^2 (25.7 ft^2) for every five arts students and one for every seven science students. Later surveys indicated that the provision of a new building leads to a higher rate of use, and confirmed that arts students tended to use the library more than science students. The working group concluded that one place for every six students overall would be appropriate, and that the area of 2.39 m^2 (or 25.7 ft^2) per reader station was adequate.

Recommendations of the report. The results of the investigations of the working group[9] were that:

- The allowance be 3.8 linear meters (or 12.47 ft) of occupied shelving per FTE student, which is 0.62 m² (or 6.67 ft²) per FTE student when translated into area.
- The amount of space provided for administration be 20% of the total area needed for books and readers.
- If one takes one reader station at 2.39 m² (or 25.7 ft²) for every six students, the following becomes the overall norm:

Seating:	0.40 m²/4.3 ft²
Bookstack:	0.62 m²/6.67 ft²
Subtotal:	1.02 m²/10.97 ft²
Administration:	0.20 m²/2.15 ft²
Total:	1.22 m²/13.12 ft²
i.e., per FTE student	1.25 m²/13.5 ft²

- Future university library building requirements should be based on the concept of a self-renewing library.
- The size of the library should be assessed by:

  - applying the norm of 1.25 m² (13.5 ft²) to the planned number of FTE students;
  - adding provision for future growth at a rate of 0.2 m² (2.15 ft²) per FTE student (projected ten years ahead);
  - adding appropriate provision for special collections.

  Only if the area calculated in this way significantly exceeds the area of the existing library will the possibility of additional space be considered.
- Space for a reserve store should be calculated to cater for the closed access storage of five years' accessions at current rates.
- Once a university's reserve store is filled, surplus stock should be sent to the British Library (Lending Division).

The UGC accepted the committee's recommendations provisionally, with the intention of further considering its policy over the next several years. However, the ensuing uproar was so great that the UGC was obliged to announce the immediate establishment of a steering group on library research. The general opinion of librarians on *The Atkinson Report* was that it was naive and too hastily prepared to be applied to what was after all a very complex problem. Bryan,[10] Librarian of the University of Sydney, in reviewing the report and its possible application to Australian libraries, called it "an extremely dangerous document, presenting as it does the apparently reasonable exposition of an extremely glib oversimplification."

Comments. A number of criticisms have been made of the report:

1. The Standing Conference of National and University Libraries (SCONUL)[11] rejected the concept of the self-renewing library on the grounds that:

   - it was a crude instrument for dealing with a complex problem;
   - it was based on inadequate research;
   - it paid too little regard to the needs of scholarship, particularly in the humanities;
   - even in economic terms, no adequate argument in favor of self-renewal was established in the document;
   - there would certainly be loss of potential donations due to the strictures placed on their prompt acceptance;
   - there was a high-level risk involved in basing the whole scheme on one national storage library, the British Library (Lending Division).

2. A concern of the working group was to establish whether it was reasonable to relate the size of the library required directly to the number of students. It then calculated the average number of linear meters of occupied shelving per FTE student and this figure became the basis of the UGC norms. No further mention was made as to whether this was in fact "reasonable," and no justification was given for using this factor.

3. Apart from a library providing for the book needs of students, the size of the bookstock need not necessarily be related to the size of the student body, except in the provision of multicopies.[12] What every library requires is a basic general collection relating to teaching and research programs, whether the university be small or large in terms of student numbers.

4. When one looks at the requirements of postgraduate research students, there is even less correlation between student numbers and bookstock because numbers are seldom large enough to require the provision of multicopies, and in addition, stock must be built up in much more depth, detail, and sophistication: "To link provision permanently with student numbers places unnecessary emphasis on undergraduate studies, and at worst infers that the library has no function in relation to research."[13]

5. In any good university library the material acquired for undergraduate use comprises a steadily decreasing proportion of the total stock. One thus limits the size of a good library by relating it directly to student numbers. Consequently many institutions will be committed to inadequacy unless their student numbers rise. *The Atkinson Report* threatens most of all those libraries remote from the major national libraries. With severe limitations on the size of their own stock and no easy access to other resources, they could cease to exist as places of serious study.

6. The report recognized that if a library became self-renewing there would be additional recurrent costs involved in selecting and moving withdrawn books, adjusting records, and fetching requested books. It stated, however, that these costs would be limited compared to those spent in cleaning and maintaining ever-growing bookstacks on open access.[14] This feeling was not shared by university librarians. Economies of storage must be set off against staffing costs. Gibb[15] mentioned in 1976 that Manchester University Library would have to employ an additional 12 senior members of staff and ancil-

lary labor at a cost of £90,000 per year to withdraw 50,000 volumes per year.

7. The great difficulty of deciding what to withdraw was recognized by the working party. However, it did not offer any helpful advice on the subject, instead referring readers to Annex H of the *Report*,[16] a note by SCONUL stating:

Loans provide in most libraries the only quantifiable indication of the use of the stock. Even then they are inaccurate guides, since a loan is only a declaration of intent. . . Few libraries will have statistics of in-library use, even though this might be more useful. Books consulted within the stacks and books treated as reference material may very well be a more valuable contribution than those borrowed.

Further information is thus needed about the way in which books are used.

8. A further difficulty resulting from withdrawal is reduction in browsing. In the humanities especially, a library is a place where ideas may be stimulated by a good collection and the chance encounter made through browsing. The Association of University Teachers[17] amplified this point: "It is not just a question of browsing. . . . It is a matter of not putting out of use materials covering a wide range of time, and not destroying completeness." In support of the UGC however, Urquhart[18] believes that the existence of subject bibliographies today more than compensates for possible loss in browsing. He suggests that the research worker should be interested in what exists on a particular topic rather than what a particular library contains on that topic.

9. Havard-Williams and Gilman[19] believe that there are widely differing stock and space requirements for different subjects and individual universities. They state that arts students usually require more books than science students. Scientists generally need up-to-date material whereas arts students may require a good deal of retrospective

material. "Therefore any policy which advocates withdrawal at a rate equal to acquisition, so bringing about a gradual updating of the stock, could possibly be penalising arts students . . . and those working in specialized fields."

10. Havard-Williams and Gilman further point out that individual universities inevitably encounter their own unique problems because of factors such as size, age, locality, and fields of teaching and research. At Essex University, for example, a year's acquisitions amounts to a high percentage of the total stock; Manchester University would incur far greater costs by storing at the British Library than locally; the librarian at Bristol University felt that the exchange of old books for new would undermine the careful building up of research collections over a long period.[20]

11. There is a substantial reduction in the space allotted to readers. By providing one place for every six FTE students, a library is supplying study space for only 16.6% of the total number of students. The majority of university libraries in Britain exceed this norm, and it seems unfortunate that one of the good standards achieved in British libraries is likely to be reduced.[21] Bryan[22] points out that as regards reader places, nearly all Australian libraries provide seating for far higher percentages of the student population. Many range between 30% and 40%, thus casting some doubt as to the usefulness of this standard.

Thus although the self-renewing library may at first seem to be a simple concept, the problems involved in putting it into practice are numerous. Even though universities are having to rethink their growth policies in view of financial cutbacks, the decision of the UGC to instruct them on how they should deal with one expensive part of their commitment, the library, was too facile a solution. The problems of university libraries in the United Kingdom are not likely to be solved by *The Atkinson Report,* as they are as varied as the universities themselves.[23] One

positive outcome of the report, however, is a greater awareness of the situation and the need to alleviate it. To this end much research is now being undertaken and alternatives to the self-renewing concept considered.

AMERICAN UNIVERSITY LIBRARY SPACE STANDARDS

In the United States, space standards grew out of circumstances similar to those in the United Kingdom. Expansion of colleges and universities in the 1950s and 1960s had resulted in enormous increases in building investment and a need for guidelines for more effective planning and use became manifest. There have been many attempts since the 1950s to establish norms and guidelines for the purposes of creating and maintaining standards, and of providing architects and librarians with very necessary help in the complex process of planning a new library building. Examples are Smith, *College and University Space Requirements* (1954); Russell and Doi, *Manual for Studies of Space Utilization in Colleges and Universities* (1957); Bareither and Schellinger, *University Space Planning* (1968); as well as Metcalf (1965), Ellsworth (1968), Havard-Williams (1970), and many others. Lynch[24] has described the early development of university library standards in the United States and the effect of the 1959 *Standards for College Libraries* on this development. A number of university librarians, impressed with the improvements in college libraries resulting from use of standards, began to consider the establishment of *university* library standards (1967). Although there was no doubt as to the desirability of standards, Lynch mentions that there were numerous difficulties encountered in their development, stemming primarily from disagreement on the definition of "university" and on whether standards should be qualitative or quantitative.[25] The 1967 attempt was initiated by the Association of College and Research Libraries. This group, with the help of the Association of Research Libraries, established a committee with Downs as Chairman, and with a mandate to complete a list of criteria that would result in excellent library service and facilities.[26] To do this, the committee selected and analyzed 50 leading university libraries, and any library could then be measured against a library or group of libraries to which it aspired. The standards given consisted primarily of concrete, quantitative data (1974).

A follow-up committee established in 1975 under the chairmanship of Smith ran into a difference of opinion on quantitative standards, and decided that comparing institutions in the ways proposed by the Downs Committee would give invalid results. It thus recommended the use of common techniques rather than quantitative standards.[27]

Another concerted effort to provide guidelines was made by the Planning and Management Division of the Western Interstate Commission for Higher Education (WICHE) in Colorado, in cooperation with the American Association of Collegiate Registrars and Admissions Officers, who jointly produced a series of manuals entitled *The Higher Education Facilities Planning and Management Manuals* (*1971*). Although this research attempted to cover the whole range of higher education activities, it did give specific attention to libraries, and provided some useful techniques of measurement.

In any planning activity it is necessary for the librarian to evaluate the capacity of existing facilities and to project future requirements. A large quantity of information must be collected before one can undertake this exercise, and the WICHE system provides a useful checklist.[28] The following information must be obtained in order to evaluate *existing* space:

• capacity of existing library stacks;
• capacity of existing library reader facilities;
• capacity of existing staff and service facilities;
• existing size of library collection in bound volumes;
• existing reader population (full-time equivalent or FTE);
• existing number of library staff requiring space;
• existing assignable square feet (ASF) of stack space;
• existing ASF of reader space;

• existing total number of reader stations;
• existing ASF of office and library processing and service space.

In addition, the following utilization assumptions (or norms) are required:

• stack density criterion expressed as bound volumes/ASF;
• percentage of FTE students to be provided with reader stations;
• average number of ASF/reader station;
• average ASF/library staff member requiring space.

The procedure uses the above information to establish utilization rates, the capacities of the various facilities, and the percentage of existing reader stations to current FTE student enrollment as opposed to the desired percentage. These evaluations can be very helpful in pointing out any imbalances in the various types of space and in indicating any excess of space in one area that could be converted to meet a need in another.

For *future* building projects, the following information is required in order to project space requirements:

• the data mentioned above regarding existing facilities;
• projected additional ASF of stack space required;
• projected additional ASF of reader space required;
• projected additional ASF of library staff and service space required;
• projected size of collection at each planning stage;
• projected reader population (FTEs) to be served at each planning stage;
• projected library staff requiring space at each planning stage;
• ASF of stack, reader and staff space expected to be in use at each planning stage.

Using this information, the projected stack space, number of reader stations, and staff and service space required at each planning stage may be calculated. The projected size of the library collection may be found by estimating expected size or by using estimated growth factors.

To assist in calculating the necessary data, unit areas have been established for the three main library space types. Unit area values vary widely with the type and density of stack shelving, the types of reader stations, and the composition and processing operations of staff and service functions, yet they provide useful guidelines to library planners.

STACK UNIT FLOOR AREAS

Table 3.1 illustrates an average situation, and relates to bound volumes (or equivalent). The University of California[30] has calculated space allowances for more specific types of library materials (Table 3.2).

Table 3.1. General Criteria for Stacks[29]

Type of stack area	Average bound volumes/ASF	Average ASF/ bound volume
Open stack reading room	8–10	0.125–0.1
Open stacks	10–12	0.1 –0.081
Closed stacks	12–15	0.083–0.067
Compact storage	40–60	0.025–0.017

Metcalf concurs with the average bookstock capacities outlined by Wheeler and Githens:[31]

Subject	Vols/foot of shelf	Vols/single-faced section
Fiction	8	168
Economics	8	168
Literature	7	147
History	7	147
Art	7	147
Technology/Science	6	126
Medicine	5	105
Govt. Pubs.	5	105
Bound Journals	5	105
Law	4	84

It is suggested that 125 volumes per single-faced unit be used for working purposes, and this is in agreement with the University of California norm mentioned above. In general, values ranged from 0.083 to 0.1 ASF/volume. If "volume" is defined as a bound volume, the value of 0.1 ASF/volume is appropriate. Lesser values are achieved by calculating "equivalent" volumes for other types of material. However, the calculation of equivalents is so complex as to be inappropriate. It is therefore suggested that a planning criterion of 0.1 ASF/bound volume be used, recognizing that this assumes a mix of library resources (0.009 ASM/bound volume is the metric equivalent).

READER STATION UNIT FLOOR AREAS

These depend largely on the type of reader station, the design of the furniture, and allowance

Table 3.2. University of California Space Norms

Type	Unit	ASF/ Unit	ASM/ Unit
Stacks (single-face section):			
Books	125 volumes	8.7	0.8
Documents, pamphlets	1,000 items	8.7	0.8
Microfilm (boxed)	400 reels	8.7	0.8
Newspapers (unbound)	7 titles	8.7	0.8
Newspapers (back files)	9 volumes	8.7	0.8
Periodicals (unbound)	15 titles	15.0	1.4
Periodicals (boxed)	30 titles	8.7	0.8
Recordings	500 records	8.7	0.8
Reference books	75 volumes	15.0	1.4
Alternate to stacks:			
Maps	1,000/case	42.0	3.9
Microfilm (reels)	400/case	11.0	1.0
Slides	5,000/case	17.0	1.6

Table 3.3. Unit Areas for Reader Stations

Type of station	ASF/station	ASM/station
Open tables and chairs	20–25	1.86–2.33
Small carrels	25–30	2.33–2.79
Research carrels (open)	30–35	2.79–3.26
Enclosed carrels	40–70	3.72–6.51
Audiovisual carrels	35–45	3.26–4.19
Typing stations	25–35	2.33–3.26
Reading lounges	25–35	2.33–3.26
Conference/seminar rooms	20–25	1.86–2.33

for internal circulation. Table 3.3 gives the average areas for various types of stations suggested in the WICHE system.[32]

Metcalf[33] sets down areas for various types of accommodation, which he stresses are approximations, but which should assist in the planning process.

Type of Station	Requirements in ft²		
	Minimum	Adequate	Generous
Lounge chair	20	25	30
Individual table	25	30	35
Tables for 4	22.5	25	27.5
Individual carrels	20	22.5	25
Double carrels	22.5	25	27.5
Enclosed carrels	30	35	40

In addition he states that more space per reader should be allowed in special areas such as typewriting rooms, areas for using audiovisual or microform materials, newspapers, archives, manuscripts, and rare books. Generally, the smaller the area of a study room the larger the area per station due to the higher proportion of internal circulation space required. A value of 25–35 ASF/station (2.33–3.26 ASM/station) is appropriate. The number of stations to be provided is determined on the basis of a policy decision made at each institution. A figure of 25% is mentioned frequently (Metcalf, California State Department, WICHE, Havard-Williams, Ellsworth). Havard-Williams[34] points out, however, that standards of accommodation are linked to standards of financial provision: "Whether you have one seat for every three students or every ten will depend on whether the financial authorities are convinced that it is an essential library service to provide seating on the scale 1 : 3 or 1 : 10."

STAFF AND SERVICE UNIT FLOOR AREAS

With regard to accommodation for library staff, Metcalf[35] mentions two points that I have frequently found to be true. In many libraries space allocated to staff tends to become inadequate before that for readers or library material. Second, library staff areas are too often congested, resulting in an environment which is not conducive to productivity. In assessing space for staff, Metcalf divides personnel into four main groups: administrative, public service, processing, and maintenance.

1. *Administrative staff.* The area allocated to this group of staff depends very much on the size of the library being considered. A library director must have adequate office space, as well as an area for meeting with members of his staff. His office may vary from 125–150 ft² (12–14 m²) in a small library to 400 ft² (40 m²) in a large one. If it does not include space for meetings, a conference room should be provided close by. Administrative staff may have officers varying from 125–250 ft² (12–25 m²), while secretarial staff will require 125 ft² (12 m²). Planners should keep in mind the need for a reception area, a stationery supply room, filing and photocopying space, computer equipment space, and (sometimes) separate restroom facilities.

2. *Public services staff.* This includes all staff who work in service areas such as circulation, reference, interlibrary loans, and information. Although much of this type of work is done from desks, heads of the various sections are likely to require offices. Metcalf[36] believes that 125 ft² (12 m²) per staff member occupying an office is a minimum allocation, as is 100 ft² (9 m²) per person on duty at any time. He emphasizes that demands for service and for a larger service staff increase each year.

3. *Processing staff.* This will include all persons involved in the ordering, receiving, cataloguing, and preparation of library materials. Metcalf[37] recommends that 100 ft² (9 m²) per person as a minimum, and preferably 125 or 150 ft² (12–14 m²) be provided, so that there is some flexibility should the staff comple-

ment increase more rapidly than anticipated or greater use of computer equipment be made. Heads of sections should be provided with an office and approximately 25 ft² (2.3 m²) more space than each of their subordinates.

4. *Maintenance staff*. Space allocated to maintenance and cleaning staff will include an area (staff room) which they may use as a base, and also space for cleaning equipment and supplies. Usually 100–125 ft² (9–12 m²) per staff member is sufficient.[38]

Havard Williams[39] describes the wide variation in standards of surface for staff. The director's office may vary from 200–400 ft² (20–40 m²), while space for processing staff may range from 60–150 ft² (5.5–14m²). He draws our attention to the fact that areas for shelving, for housing a variety of equipment, and room for movement and circulation required by staff members add to their spatial needs, and concludes that "an allowance of 120 sq. ft. or 11 m² per member of library staff should be made, including an area for an appropriate number of staff envisaged as necessary for development of the library during the period for which the building is planned." The University of California[40] has established unit area allowances for staff work stations as shown in Table 3.4.

In the California approach, an additional 5% is added to the sum of all calculated stack, reader, and staff work areas to allow for additional

Table 3.4. Unit Areas for Staff Work Stations

Staff work areas	ASF/work station	ASM/work station
Acquisitions	100	9.30
Administration	120	11.16
Bindery preparation	250	23.25
Cataloguing	110	10.23
Circulation	120	11.16
Data processing	120	11.16
Interlibrary loans	100	9.30
Periodicals	120	11.16
Photocopying	100	9.30
Receiving and mail	300	27.90
Reference	120	11.16
Special collections	120	11.16
Staff room	25	2.33
Typing pool	75	7.00

service facilities such as lobby, public catalogues, and display and storage space. The total staff and service facilities of a library may be expected to range from 25% (for a smaller library) to 18% (for a larger library) of the combined stack and reader floor area.

COMMENTS

Although procedures for the evaluation and projection of space are a useful aid to planners, they are not entirely satisfactory. They tend to ignore the enormous differences among academic fields of study in terms of their relative reliance on library materials and the scope of collections needed to support them. They also obscure differences in student characteristics and academic programs at different institutions.

Projections for future growth depend on a number of factors such as the state of the collection in certain subject fields, the rate of obsolescence, possible development of new courses, changes in educational techniques, various rates of publication in different fields, and the financial resources of the individual library. Due to the complexity of these combined factors, projection is usually done on the basis of average percentage increase in the number of volumes acquired (and removed) annually.

The number of readers to be accommodated in a library also varies widely with the institution. The frequently mentioned standard of 25% obscures diversity of library use generated by different types of courses as well as by types of readers—e.g. many law schools in the United States require that seating be provided for up to 65% of the student enrollment; a residential university may require provision for 35–40%; while a commuting university may need only 20%. Despite standards, financial limitations may prevent a university from providing the desired amount of reader accommodation in its library. In projecting reader station requirements one needs to look carefully at the user population. The authors of the WICHE project suggest that a combination of the projected student population by level of student and field of study, the distribution of faculties, and other user demands (e.g. public), may be taken as a basis for estimating demand for library reader facilities.[41]

It is accepted that in size, content, and scope of functions, the range of variance among libraries is as great as that among the colleges and universities themselves. However, physical facilities are one of the major considerations in the higher education decision-making process, and it is desirable that decisions regarding both the current operations and future directions of the institution be made with the benefit of accurate and comprehensive information in this area. In the evaluation of existing library space and in the projection of future space requirements, generally accepted unit areas play an important role, and it is in this respect that standards achieve their main purpose. At neither the state nor the national level are universities and colleges forced to adhere to specified standards.

South African University Library Space Standards

Although certain norms were applied in library buildings in South Africa as early as 1930, until 1979 there were no space standards as such that could be used as guidelines by university planners and administrators. In the past, standardized procedures were typically based on extensive analysis of historical data, and from these, national averages were derived. Against these, data from individual universities were compared and evaluated. However, the use of averages masks individual differences, and assumes that these variations above and below the average are invalid. To overcome these deficiencies, a need was felt for a planning system based on what is desirable and necessary rather than on what is or has been. The Department of National Education decided to institute the South African Post-Secondary Education Information System (SAPSE) in an attempt to provide institutions of higher education with a methodology for effective planning, and itself with the necessary information for realistic financing of these institutions. Systems in a number of countries were studied and the American system mentioned above—the WICHE *Higher Education Facilities Planning and Management Manuals*—was found to be most adaptable to local conditions. The different components were developed locally by groups of experts drawn from the universities themselves. The resulting manuals were issued initially as review editions, and input from the various universities has been encouraged in an effort to establish the most acceptable system possible.

BUILDING AND SPACE INFORMATION

The SAPSE system consists of a series of manuals, and it is those relating to space and buildings that have a direct effect on the planning of library buildings at universities. They are:

1. *Building and Space Inventory and Classification Manual* (No. 009), which is concerned with the classification systems necessary for describing and quantifying buildings and space in terms that are meaningful for planning and resource allocation.[42]
2. *Nation-Wide Space and Cost Norms for Buildings and Land Improvements other than Buildings* (No. 101), which describes a system of space and cost norms based on detailed student numbers, which will assist in planning and in providing a basis on which requests for funding may be more easily evaluated.[43]

CLASSIFICATION OF SPACE

In analyzing the space within a given building, three area measurements may be determined:

1. *Gross area:* the sum of all floor areas of the building based on exterior dimensions.
2. *Assignable area:* the sum of all the area in all rooms that may be used by the occupants to carry out their functions.
3. *Nonassignable area:* the sum of circulation, custodial, mechanical, and structural areas.

It is the assignable area that is classified into categories according to space use for analytical purposes. Following the American WICHE system, the SAPSE system divides library space up into office space and study space. Where there is doubt, allocation to a space category should be done on the basis of dominant use, e.g. academic staff study rooms in libraries are coded as study space. However, if academic staff members have been assigned such rooms as their main offices, the space is coded as office space. Librarians should note too that included under "library services" are collections in academic departments, cataloguing and indexing services separate from library collections, and the provision of study areas separate from the library, e.g. in halls of residence. It is thus important that the librarian ascertain what space on campus is recorded under library space.[44]

The SAPSE space norms are based on present or projected numbers of FTE students. In calculating space for a proposed library building, it is necessary to obtain the projected FTE student number for a specific year in the future from the university's administration. This figure is multiplied by the SAPSE space norm, and the result is the area permitted by the SAPSE system for the proposed library. Existing building space also has to be tested against the norms, with the reutilization of space, if necessary, to ensure as far as possible conformity within the SAPSE requirements.[45]

SPACE NORMS APPLICABLE TO LIBRARIES[46]

Office and conference space. When planning new buildings, the norm for office and conference space is multiplied by the anticipated number of FTE students for the year for which the building is being planned. The norm is expressed in the following formula:

$$\frac{B}{R} = \frac{\text{ASM allowed/FTE staff member}}{\text{FTE students/FTE staff member}}$$

$$= \frac{15 \text{ ASM/FTE staff member}}{65 \text{ FTE students/FTE staff member}}$$

$$= 0.213 \text{ ASM/FTE student (or 2.29 ASF/FTE student)}$$

This is a comprehensive norm for all office and conference space. To assist planners, the norm 15 ASM/FTE staff member (or 160 ASF/FTE staff member) should be utilized within the overall area allocation. Libraries may use the area available according to their individual requirements, e.g. more space may be given to tearooms and conference rooms, and less to individual offices.

Reading study space (refer to Table 3.5). The norm is expressed in the following formula:

$$\frac{A \times C}{U} = \frac{\text{ASM/study station} \times \text{annual contact hours/FTE student}}{800 \text{ potential annual contact use hours/study station}}$$

$$= \frac{2.5 \times 200}{800}$$

$$= 0.625 \text{ ASM/FTE student (or 6.73 ASF/FTE student)}$$

This norm is applicable to all study levels. Provision is made within this norm for study stations for 25% of the FTE student number, with an average of 2.5 ASM/station (±27 ASF/station).

In planning new buildings, 0.625 ASM is multiplied by the projected FTE student number for which the building is being planned, and this provides the area permitted in terms of SAPSE for study space. In South Africa, librarians are concerned that within this norm insufficient provision has been made for the use of audiovisual and computer equipment, which require more space than the traditional reader station.

Stack space (refer to Table 3.1). The SAPSE space norm may be expressed by the following formula:

$$S \times V = \text{ASM stack space/bound volume} \times \text{number of bound volumes/FTE student}$$

with values and norms per course level as shown on Table 3.6.

The planning criterion of 0.009 ASM/bound volume is used with the recognition that it implies a mix of library resources (0.1 ASF/bound volume is the imperial equivalent). For planning purposes it is necessary to have the projected number of FTE students *per course level*, and to multiply these figures by the norm. The result

Table 3.5. SAPSE Norms for the Calculation of Study and Stack Space

The ASM reading/study space per study station (A); the annual utilization hours per study station (U); the annual student study space contact hours per FTE student of a particular aggregate of course levels (C); the ASM stack space per bound volume (S); and the number of bound volumes per FTE student of a particular aggregate of course levels (V).

Course Levels*	A	U	C	S	V
2–5	2.5	800	200	0.009	60
6	2.5	800	200	0.009	120
7–10	2.5	800	200	0.009	180

*Course levels
  Levels 2–5 : Undergraduate
  Level 6   : Lower postgraduate (honors)
  Levels 7–10 : Master's and doctoral

Source: SAPSE 101 (1982), p.2.15.

Table 3.7

Course level	Reading ASM	Stack ASM	Total reading + stack	Norm-ASM/FTE (7% reading + stack)
2–5	0.625	0.540	1.165	0.082
6	0.625	1.080	1.705	0.119
7–10	0.625	1.620	2.245	0.157

will be the area for bookstacks permitted by the SAPSE system.

The linking of the norm for stack space to FTE student numbers has been questioned by librarians. This enables a university library to reach its "SAPSE limit" either because it has a collection that has been built up over many years (the older residential universities), or because student numbers have stabilized. In either case a zero-growth situation may arise: "As the national bookstock is not necessarily sufficient both qualitatively and quantitatively, the wisdom of restricting the growth of university libraries in this way is debatable."[47]

Processing space. This type of space includes catalogues, circulation desks, and storage areas for audiovisual equipment. The norm is calculated as 7% of the sum of reading and stack space.

To determine the space required for processing in a proposed library, the projected FTE student number *per course level* is multiplied by the norm. Bookbinding is sometimes included in processing space, but may also be classified under "workshop" space elsewhere in the system, in which case it should not be included in library space.[48] Space allocated to processing functions varies enormously from one library to another. Flexibility is permitted as long as the overall norm is not exceeded.

Overall space norm. When planning new libraries, the overall norm for library space may be utilized to provide the architect with the total area permitted. This allows flexibility in the subdivision and application of space according to the librarian's requirements.

Any building will have assignable and nonassignable space. SAPSE norms are applicable only to assignable space, i.e. office, reading, stack, service, and processing space. The layout of library space and the percentage ASM allocated to each space type is left to the individual librarian, with the proviso that (a) the overall ASMs do not exceed the norm, and (b) an attempt is made to maintain a ratio of 80% assignable space to 20% nonassignable space.

Comments. The positive aspect of space norms is that they allow the planner to work within finite parameters, which makes the task easier. But standards do not really make provision for

Table 3.6

Course level	Values	Norms
2–5	0.009 ASM/vol. × 60 vols.	= 0.540 ASM/FTE student
6	0.009 ASM/vol. × 120 vols.	= 1.080 ASM/FTE student
7–10	0.009 ASM/vol. × 180 vols.	= 1.620 ASM/FTE student

Table 3.8. Global Norm

Course level	ASM/FTE student	ASF/FTE student
2–5	1.478	15.91
6	2.055	22.12
7–10	2.633	28.34

the wide variety of needs within libraries. Many volumes require a lot more space than 0.009 m² (0.1 ft²); some staff members require larger offices than 15 m² (160 ft²), especially if their jobs require interaction with equipment. Automated equipment also results in larger user work stations, e.g. a person working with a microfiche reader or television monitor requires more space than one working with a book. For the new technologies, standards tend to be less than applicable.[49] Although the SAPSE norms are supposed to be formulated so as not to infringe upon the autonomy of the institution concerned, the authors do admit that they are conservative.[50]

Many of the criticisms leveled at the space restrictions imposed on university libraries in the United Kingdom by the UGC may also be applied to the SAPSE system in South Africa. Any university library that has its size determined by the number of FTE students registered with the institution is bound to find ultimately that the growth in the stock exceeds growth in student numbers and that a critical point in terms of space has been (or will be) reached. At this stage there is likely to be little choice but to remove lesser-used material from the library to storage. Although the Department of National Education does not use the term *self-renewal* at any stage in the SAPSE manuals, the concept is implicit.

The limitation on the size of a library in terms of space and consequently in terms of stock will ultimately have grave consequences for university libraries in South Africa, with its obvious local disadvantages for the research worker. First there is the problem of distance from the sources of book supply and from the great library collections of Europe and the United States, and also the distances between libraries within the country. Second, there is a lack of supplementary library facilities on any worthwhile scale. South

Africa does not have numerous large and well-stocked city libraries, nor does it have the equivalent of the British Library or the Library of Congress. Thus restricting size could create problems for the academic community.

Although much may be gained from a library that is limited to containing those items actually used, and that does not bewilder a prospective user with shelf upon shelf of "needless" material, librarians in South Africa must look at the total resources of the country in terms of research. If most of the resources research workers need cannot be obtained relatively quickly and easily from their own or nearby libraries, enormous frustration will result, and it is in this important area that South Africa suffers an isolation unknown to European or American researchers.

Summary. Although it is generally accepted that there is a need for space standards, their development and utilization are not without difficulties. As Havard-Williams[51] states, one of the major difficulties about providing standards for university library buildings is that answers vary throughout the world to the questions: (1) What is the function of a university? (2) What is the function of a university library? and (3) What purposes are served by a university library building? A library building and the allocation of space within it will be a reflection of how a particular librarian responds to these questions. Inevitably there is disagreement on definition as well as differences in emphasis. There is such a great variety of libraries that many believe standards serve no purpose. Private or research institutions with generous financing will have little or no need for "minimum" facilities, while institutions undergoing financial cutbacks will provide the best they can in the circumstances, despite the standards. In both the United Kingdom and South Africa, university library accommodation is considered in space norms relating not to the library exclusively, but also to library or study space contained elsewhere in the university. Problems such as these cast doubt on whether standards provide a satisfactory aid to library planning. It seems that standards are inevitably a compromise, and they should be recognized as such. They should be used as guidelines, as a tool in the planning process, and as a baseline from which individual situations may be assessed. Their major usefulness lies in providing a framework for evaluation.

The IFLA Standards for University Libraries[52] contain a statement on "facilities" that are qualitative rather than quantitative, and that embody the spirit of standards as "a means by which the quality of the library serving a university can be assessed ... and a framework within which various countries or regions could develop their own statements of standards."

The standard reads as follows:[53]

- The buildings housing the university's libraries should be of sufficient size and quality to house the collection and to provide sufficient space for their use by students, faculty and staff.
- The facilities should be attractive and designed to promote operational efficiencies and effectiveness of use. Specific factors include layout of the buildings, light, ventilation, temperature and humidity control, stacks, exhibit areas, number of reader stations.
- Suitable space for staff must be available.
- Within the context of the university's educational purposes, the library should be well-equipped to encourage maximum use by the university's students, faculty and staff.

COMPARATIVE STANDARDS

METRIC/IMPERIAL CONVERSION

$$
\begin{aligned}
1 \text{ ft}^2 &= 0.093 \text{ m}^2 \\
1 \text{ m}^2 &= 10.764 \text{ ft}^2 \\
1 \text{ ft} &= 0.305 \text{ m} \\
1 \text{ m} &= 3.281 \text{ ft} \\
1 \text{ lb} &= 0.454 \text{ kg} \\
1 \text{ kg} &= 2.205 \text{ lbs}
\end{aligned}
$$

- The generally accepted minimum work surface per reader is 0.90 m × 0.60 m (3 ft × 2 ft).
- Height from floor = 0.76m (2' 6").

Table 3.8. Study Accommodation

Country/origin	Under-graduate	Post-graduate	Research	% enrollment
U.S.A.	25ft² (2.3m²)	35ft² (3.3m²)	55ft² (5.0m²)	25–30
Canada	25ft² (2.3m²)	35ft² (3.3m²)	75ft² (7.0m²)	25–40
U.K.	26ft² (2.39m²)	26ft² (2.39m²)	— —	16
France	16ft² (1.5m²)	16ft² (1.5m²)	65ft² (6.0m²)	10 (science) 12 (arts)
S.A.	27ft² (2.5m²)	37ft² (3.5m²)	37ft² (3.5m²)	25

- Height of chair seat = 0.25m (10ins) lower than the table.
- Graduates will require larger work surfaces.
- Area for reader's chair = 0.90 × 0.75m (3ft × 2' 6").
- If one allows for aisles around desks, average space required for 1 reader station = 2.3m² (25ft²).

Table 3.9. Stack Space

Country/origin	Open access	Storage
U.S.A.	10 vols./ft² (108 vols./m²)	15 vols./ft² (160 vols./m²)
Canada	10 vols./ft² (108 vols./m²)	12.5 vols./ft² (135 vols./m²)
U.K. (books)	20 vols./ft² (213 vols./m²)	23 vols./ft² (248 vols./m²)
U.K. (journals)	10 vols./ft² (106 vols./m²)	11.3 vols./ft² (122 vols./m²)
France	15.4 vols./ft² (166 vols./m²)	—
S.A.	10.3 vols./ft² (110 vols./m²)	—

All standards assume shelving in bays of 7' 6" high × 3ft long × 8ins wide (2.3m × 0.915m × 0.2m).

FLOOR LOADING

150lbs/ft² (750kg/m²)

LIBRARY STAFF SPACE

In general, senior library personnel are allocated between 160ft² and 270ft² (15m²–25m²). Processing staff/assistant librarians: 100ft²–120ft² (9m²–11m²). Secretarial/clerical staff: 75ft²–100ft² (7m²–9m²).

REFERENCES

1. Western Interstate Commission for Higher Education, National Center for Higher Education Management Systems, *Higher Education Facilities Inventory and Classification Manual,* Technical Report 36 (Boulder, Colo.: WICHE, 1972), p.1.
2. D.K. Halstead, *Statewide Planning in Higher Education* (Washington, D.C.: U.S. Department of Health, Education, and Welfare, 1974), p.419.
3. International Federation of Library Associations, Section of Public Libraries, *Standards for Public Libraries* (Munich: Verlag Dokumentation, 1973), p.11.
4. P. Havard-Williams, "Standards of surface needed for university libraries," *Libri,* vol.21, no.4, p.374.

UNITED KINGDOM

5. H. Faulkner-Brown, "Academic library buildings in the United Kingdom," *Advances in Librarianship,* vol.3 (New York: Seminar Press, 1972), p.110.
6. University Grants Committee, *Capital Provision for University Libraries,* Report of a Working Party (London: HMSO, 1976), annex C, p.26.
7. Ibid., p.5.
8. Ibid., pp.7–12.
9. Ibid., p.13.
10. H. Bryan, "The perpetuation of inadequacy: a comment on the Atkinson Report," *Australian Academic and Research Libraries,* vol.7, 1976, p.220.
11. Standing Conference of National and University Libraries, quoted by Bryan, p.219.
12. Bryan, p.215.
13. Ibid.
14. University Grants Committee, p.11.
15. F. Gibb, "Universities will fight to shelve Atkinson plan for libraries," *Times Educational Supplement,* no.271, December 1976, p.5.
16. Standing Conference of National and University Libraries, quoted in University Grants Committee, annex H, p.40.
17. Association of University Teachers, quoted by P. Havard-Williams and A. Gilman, *International Library Review,* vol.10, 1978, p.55.
18. D.J. Urquhart, quoted by P. Havard-Williams and A. Gilman, ibid.
19. P. Havard-Williams and A. Gilman, "The self-

renewing library," *International Library Review,* vol.10, 1978, p.56.
20. Ibid., p.57.
21. Bryan, p.217.
22. Ibid., p.218.
23. S.J. Teague, "British university libraries today," *New Library World,* vol.79, no.931, January 1978, p.37.

UNITED STATES

24. B.P. Lynch, "University library standards," *Library Trends,* Summer 1982, p.33.
25. Ibid.
26. Ibid., p.35.
27. Ibid., p.38.
28. Western Interstate Commission for Higher Education, "Planning and Management Systems Division," *Higher Education Facilities Planning and Management, Manual Four,* Technical Report, 17-4 (Boulder, Colo.: WICHE, 1971), p.12.
29. Ibid., p.60.
30. University of California, Berkeley, Office of the President, "University of California Planning Guide for Libraries: Unit Area Allowances" (1968), in Western Interstate Commission for Higher Education, Technical Report, 17-4, p.61.
31. J.L. Wheeler and A.M. Githens, quoted by K.D. Metcalf, *Planning Academic and Research Library Buildings* (New York: McGraw Hill, 1965), p.393.
32. Western Interstate Commission for Higher Education, p.62.
33. Metcalf, pp.129, 392.
34. Havard-Williams, p.376.
35. Metcalf, p.129.
36. Ibid., p.130.
37. Ibid., p.131.
38. Ibid., p.132.
39. Havard-Williams, pp.383–84.
40. University of California, p.63.
41. Western Interstate Commission for Higher Education, Technical Report, 17-4, p.7.

SOUTH AFRICA

42. Manual 009, *Building and Space Inventory and Classification Manual,* a local adaptation of the *Higher Education Facilities Inventory and Classification Manual,* Western Interstate Commission for Higher Education (WICHE) (Boulder, Colo.: U.S. Department of Health, Education, and Welfare, 1974).
43. Manual 101, *Nation-Wide Space and Cost Norms for Buildings and Land Improvements Other Than Build-*

ings, an adaptation of part of Manual VI of the series *Higher Education Facilities Planning and Management Manuals,* WICHE (Boulder, Colo.: U.S. Department of Health, Education, and Welfare, 1971).

44. *Riglyne by die Toepassing van SANSO-Bounorme van Biblioteke van Suid-Afrikaanse Residensiele Universiteite.* Opgestel deur Biblioteekdienste, Universiteit van Suid-Afrika en Universiteit van Pretoria (Pretoria: University of South Africa, 1984), p.6 [unpublished].
45. Ibid., p.1.
46. Ibid., pp.10–21.
47. Ibid., p.17.
48. Ibid., p.19.
49. E. Cohen and A. Cohen, *Automation, Space Management and Productivity: A Guide for Libraries* (New York: Bowker, 1981), p.91.
50. *South African Post-Secondary Education Nation-Wide Space and Cost Norms for Buildings and Land Improvements Other than Buildings,* Manual 101, p.i.
51. P. Havard-Williams, "Standards of surface needed for university libraries," *Libri,* vol.21, no.4, p.374.
52. B.P. Lynch (ed.), "Standards for university libraries," *IFLA Journal,* vol.13, no.2, 1987, p.121.
53. Ibid., p.124.

4 United Kingdom: Case Studies

Although more academic libraries have been constructed in the last 25 years than at any other time, it has not automatically followed that buildings have become progressively better. The architectural extravagances of the first half of the century had given way by the 1950s and 1960s to the relative simplicity of modular design, resulting in libraries that were flexible, functional, and less expensive to construct and maintain than their predecessors. Although these modular libraries achieved a functional excellence that has been difficult to improve upon, many people became bored with their uniformly rectangular style, and in recent years there has been a noticeable trend toward reintroducing the dramatic, the aesthetic, and the symbolic into library design. Unless very carefully handled by a sensitive architect, this has tended to reduce the usefulness and increase the cost of academic library buildings.

The case studies that appear in this chapter and in chapters 5 and 6 review selected libraries in three countries—the United Kingdom, the United States, and South Africa. Although all are fine examples of library planning, in some instances an attempt by the architect or the planning team to "make a statement" has reduced the overall efficiency of the building. Library planners must learn to be as aware of these possible pitfalls as they are of the more generally known desirable features such as flexibility, security, accessibility, and functional layout.

EDINBURGH UNIVERSITY LIBRARY

Architects:	Sir Basil Spence, Glover, and Ferguson (Edinburgh)
Floor areas:	Gross total area—27,720 m² (300,000 ft²)
	Total usable area—20,006 m² (215,000 ft²)
	Balance area—7,714 m² (85,000 ft²)
Accommodation:	Book capacity—±2 million vols.
	Reader stations—2,500
	Staff—114
Costs:	Building cost—£1,700,655
	Furniture/equipment—£400,900
	Total—£2,101,555
	Cost/m² (unfurnished)—£61
Date opened:	September 1967
Librarian:	E.R.S. Fifoot

The university library was founded in 1580 when Clement Litil, a local advocate, died, bequeathing his collection of 300 books to "the Toun and Kirk of Edinburgh."[1] From this collection, of which 276 books remain, the library has grown to its present size of well over 1.6 million items, housed in the main and several branch libraries.

In 1961–62 the university's requirements for a new main library were stated in a substantial brief, which was expanded and modified in the course of planning and in the light of the developing activities of the University Grants Committee (UGC). The plans were passed before restrictive measures were introduced, and thus the Edinburgh University Library was not limited financially or in any other way.

SITE AND ACCESS

Edinburgh University, like many British universities of its age, is scattered over the city, although there are concentrations of university buildings at George Square and King's Buildings. The library is located on the southwest corner of George Square, of which it commands a beautiful view. Unfortunately an old university building had to be demolished to make way for the library—an unpopular decision with many of Edinburgh's citizens, but one cannot deny that the library occupies an ideal site. Although very large, certain restrictions placed on the building by the planning authorities of the city and the university have ensured that it does not

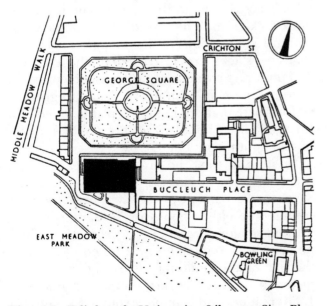

Fig. 4.1. Edinburgh University Library: Site Plan. *Source: Architects' Journal,* Information Library, 19 June 1968. SFB (97), p. 1392. By permission from Peter Carolin, Editor.

dominate the area to any great extent. The city authorities enforced a height restriction which, when coupled with the floor area and the curtilage of the site, dictated the massing of the building.[2] New buildings adjoining the library were already designed with a strong horizontal emphasis. Restrictions were also placed on the external finishes of the library to achieve uniformity with its surroundings. Vehicular access is via Buccleuch Place and George Square Lane, while pedestrian access tends to be primarily from George Square itself and the university buildings surrounding it. (See site plan, Fig. 4.1.)

EXTENDIBILITY

The *Brief*[3] stated that the building should be planned such that an extension could readily be attached to the southeast side. Thus there were to be no permanent obstacles to expansion such as stairwells, lifts, or toilets at this point. However, it is very unlikely that Edinburgh University Library will ever be extended. In terms of present UGC standards, it contains an extremely generous amount of space. With the library expected to serve for about 70 years, it will be some time before self-renewal becomes a reality at Edinburgh.

FLEXIBILITY

The library was planned and built to be the main library of the campus for the foreseeable future. As it is difficult to forecast the development of a university or the pattern of library use very far in advance, and considering that technological changes will in all certainty alter the character of library services, it was emphasized in the *Brief* that "the planning of the building be modular with load bearing columns at regular intervals, that no load bearing interior walls be constructed, that all ceilings have uniform heights, and all floors be capable of bearing stack weights." The major need for flexibility also required that the bulk of each floor should fit exactly and without horizontal voids over the floor below. Fenestration and the siting of stairwells and lifts

Fig. 4.2. Edinburgh University Library: View of Exterior

were also to be such that interior rearrangements could easily be made.[4]

Adaptability—the freedom to interchange book storage areas with reader areas and other work places while still maintaining optimum conditions for each—is one of the main features of the Edinburgh University Library. The module size is 8.4 m (27 ft), and this allows complete freedom of bookstack layout in either direction with stack centers at a choice of 1.17 m, 1.35 m, 1.65 m, and 2.06 m (3' 10", 4' 6", 5' 5", and 6' 9" respectively).[5] The uniformly distributed load is 10.7 kN/m² (220 lbs/ft²), which could allow for compact shelving throughout. Very few libraries today can afford floor loading of this strength; 7 kN/m² (150 lbs/ft²) is the norm. Should it become necessary in the future, this library will thus be able to greatly increase its capacity without major structural alterations.

Flexibility is also affected by ventilation, temperature control, lighting, and ceiling height. Although Edinburgh University Library has full air conditioning throughout, flexibility has been restricted by the combination of a 2.44 m (8 ft)-high ceiling (the generally accepted height is 2.59 m or 8' 6") and fixed continuous recessed fluorescent lighting in strips at 1.35 m centers (4' 5") across the width of the building along bookstack aisles. The tops of the bookstacks are within 152 mm (6ins) of the ceiling, which means that the stacks are restricted to the direction and position in which they are presently placed so as to maintain an even distribution of light. It is unfortunate that this building, planned and built for flexibility, should have this quality reduced by the lighting system.

In spite of this, the architect has achieved a great measure of success as regards flexibility. Seventy-five percent of the floor area could accommodate either books or readers efficiently without major alteration—a particularly high percentage. Adaptability was tested early on in the life of the building. The original requirement was that the library should accommodate 1,850 readers and 2 million volumes.[6] The subsequent rapid expansion of the university caused the requirement for reader places to be increased to 2,500, and this was achieved at the

GROUND FLOOR PLAN

Fig. 4.3. Edinburgh University Library: Floor Plan, Ground Level. *Source:* Sir Basil Spence, Glover and Ferguson, Architects (Edinburgh). "Edinburgh University Library" (1968). By permission from James Beveridge of Sir Basil Spence, Glover and Ferguson.

expense of a small proportion of the stack capacity but without any structural alterations.

FLOOR LAYOUT

The lower ground floor houses the mechanical plant rooms, photographic department, bindery, staff room, an immense covered loading bay, and closed access stack areas. At the front of the building on this level, with access from the main entrance, is a readers' coffee room.

The ground floor accommodates various library services such as the control desk, service desk and catalogues, main reference room, current periodicals, rare books department, and an open plan work area for technical processing departments (see Fig. 4.3). The first floor houses the central administration of the library, a committee room, the undergraduate reading room, and the photocopying room. Because the entrance foyer on the ground floor is double height, the arrangement of the first floor is restricted and the layout consequently somewhat confusing.

On the second floor is the reading room housing the main collection of textbooks for first- and second-year students in the arts and social sciences. There is also a listening room for the library's collection of audio recordings.

The third, fourth, and fifth floors of the building all have study and research accommodation in the form of tables, open carrels, and closed study and typing rooms. The sixth floor is a closed access area, housing theses and a number of special collections.

COMPACTNESS

The Edinburgh University Library is compact. It is a large rectangle approximately 76.25 m long and 45.75 m wide (250 ft × 150 ft), with eight floors. The main user core is toward the center of the building on each level, with additional staircases on either side. Internal movement is thus straightforward and travel distances have been kept as short as possible. However, the library is large, and despite correct placing of lifts

and staircases, distances from one part of the building to another are great. The librarian in charge of building and planning[7] feels that the library is too big. The desire of the planning team not to underestimate the size of the building has possibly led to overcompensation.

ORGANIZATION

The circulation and information desks are centrally placed and immediately obvious on entering the library. Vertical circulation routes are central and easy to locate on each floor. Above the main floor the arrangement of major library elements is repetitive. Thus even though it is a large library, readers are generally able to find their way around the building without too much difficulty.

VARIETY

Reader accommodation comprises approximately 1,300 seats in the first- and second-floor reading rooms, consisting primarily of single tables in large groups within the stack area; 200 open carrels on the perimeter of the various floors; 40 typing carrels; 20 study rooms; and further seats scattered over the stack floors in "oases" and along the peripheries. The remaining reader stations are in the various reference rooms, the current periodical room, and the manuscript and rare books department. There is a wide variety of seating, much of it of excellent quality. The design of the open carrels is particularly successful, comprising a substantial work surface with a cupboard below and bookshelf above, each fitted with a power point and provided with a wastepaper basket (see Fig. 4.5). Research carrels are also well designed. In addition to a work surface with a drawer below, there is sound proofing, a side table for a typewriter, a table lamp, power point, wastepaper basket, and two chairs.

The *Brief* to the architect specifically requested that "reading rooms should not be of the monumental kind, but rather a series of areas not necessarily uniform in size, screened by

TYPICAL UPPER FLOOR PLAN

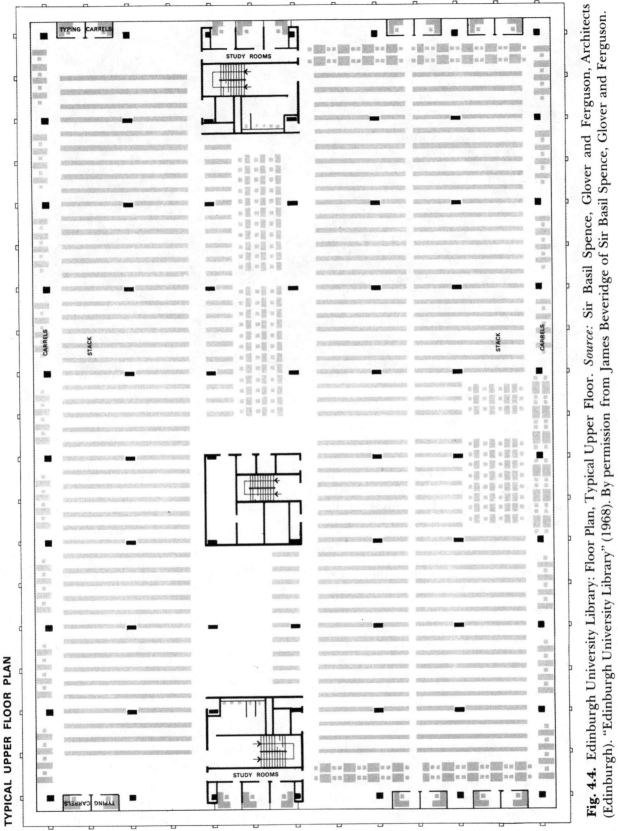

Fig. 4.4. Edinburgh University Library: Floor Plan, Typical Upper Floor. *Source:* Sir Basil Spence, Glover and Ferguson, Architects (Edinburgh). "Edinburgh University Library" (1968). By permission from James Beveridge of Sir Basil Spence, Glover and Ferguson.

Fig. 4.5. Edinburgh University Library: Study Carrel

shelving or other furniture."[8] However, reading areas at Edinburgh do tend to be larger than one finds in the newer (and smaller) university libraries in Britain today, and they are not very successful. Possibly this is related to the overall size of the library, but much could be gained if attention were given to rearranging the reading/stack areas into smaller, more intimate spaces. Of three seminar rooms provided initially, only one is used for this purpose currently. The others are used to house special collections.

COMFORT

The usefulness of library spaces is determined to some extent by the physical conditions that exist in them. There are several aspects to be considered, ranging from comfort of library users and staff to the need for preservation of rare manuscripts. As regards heating and ventilation, the following physical conditions are regarded as ideal:

Temperature: 20.6°C (±1.7°C) or 69°F (±5°F)
Relative humidity: 45%–55%
Air change: Minimum of four changes per hour
Air filtration: Filtration should be effective against particle size in excess of one micron. In industrial areas air washers should be used.

Edinburgh University tries to maintain a temperature of 20°C (68°F) and a relative humidity of 55%. There are five air changes per hour. Filtration is to a five-micron size, and in addition an air washer is used.[9]

The library has full-height double glazing on all sides, which is largely an attempt to relieve the claustrophobic effect of large floor areas and low ceilings. Care has been taken to control heat gain and consequent discomfort to readers from direct sunlight on this glass, and each floor projects 1.37 m (4' 6") beyond the face of the window to form a continuous balcony. In addition, there is heat-absorbing glass on the south face, and fixed louvers on the east and west faces. In winter, additional heating is provided around the periphery of the building.[10] Despite all these precautions, the large window areas produce considerable variation in temperature between reading stations on the south and north sides of the library. Air conditioning helps to counteract temperature fluctuation, but as mentioned earlier, breakdowns occur, causing serious problems in a building of this size.

The library has good overall lighting. Illumination levels are 380–430 lux at the work surface, and 130–160 lux on the vertical surface of the bookstacks. The fittings are fixed, recessed fluorescent tubes combined with the air conditioning ducting. Somewhat unimaginative, they form continuous strips across the building. The full-height windows on all sides of the building allow much natural light to enter the peripheral areas. However, on the south side there is a certain amount of glare and dazzle, especially in winter, despite the use of tinted glass. In many areas there is also a problem with reflected glare caused by polished desk surfaces and linoleum flooring.

To lessen visual and aural disturbance, "activity" areas are separated from quiet reading areas and sound-absorbing materials are used on floors, walls, and ceilings. The entrance and circulation desk area is closed off from all other areas. The lift lobby within the central core is divided from the two undergraduate reading rooms by glazed partitions. Groups of readers are isolated from the core and from each other by the stacks. To further reduce noise, acoustic ceiling tiles are used throughout the building, and carpeting is used on the two undergraduate levels. On stack floors, carpeting is laid within reading areas only; the linoleum flooring used elsewhere produces less noise than expected. Finally, fixed double glazing prevents the entry of outside noise. Although it is a large building with many occupants, there is little disturbance to the individual.

CONSTRUCTION AND MATERIALS

The building has eight floors, the eighth being considerably smaller than the others and thus not visible from ground level. The structure is faced with precast concrete, finished with a veneer of portland stone. Concrete columns and balcony soffits have been left as struck from the shutter, with a smooth finish. Inside, the main concourse is clad and furnished in teak, with a quartzite floor. All other areas are finished in white beech or plaster, with carpeted or linoleum floors.[11] The extensive use of wood in furnishings, paneling, and staircases is most attractive. It wears well, is easy to maintain, and gives the library a feeling of luxury.

ASSESSMENT

1. This was one of the first libraries of its size in the United Kingdom to be fully air conditioned (seven of the eight floors are close to an acre in size). At the time the library opened, the air conditioning was reportedly excellent throughout. Today, temperature and humidity control is unsatisfactory, and problems with condensation are encountered in winter.

2. The immense main concourse, two floors high and dominated by large concrete pillars 915 mm × 460 mm (3' × 1' 6") is not successful. The circulation and information desks become insignificant in an area of this magnitude, and the general impression gained on entering the library is of a daunting and somewhat unwelcoming building. The large central staircase, though beautifully constructed, adds to this initial impression. Possibly more care should have been taken by the architects to make this area more friendly and less imposing. Its monumental proportions do not achieve anything positive.

3. The design team used the cost limit optimally by creating a large enclosed area with small perimeter ratio (i.e. a rectangle) and minimal internal subdivisions. The "savings" on structure were used on the interior finishes and

Fig. 4.6. Edinburgh University Library: Acquisitions Department

services, which are of good quality throughout.

4. Compared with a number of university libraries in the United Kingdom, Edinburgh University Library has particularly attractive staff areas (see Fig. 4.6). This is a pleasant change from the restricted and overcrowded staff conditions seen in so many recent buildings. The technical processing area with its large windows and beautiful views is most attractive, and the administration offices on the first floor are tastefully and luxuriously finished. The high-quality carpeting, good lighting, acoustic ceilings, and the sound insulation qualities of the beechwood strip partitions help to achieve this.

5. It is unfortunate that, despite the severe height restrictions imposed on the building by the planning authority, extra height could not have been given to the 2.44 m (8 ft)-high stack and reading room ceilings. This would have increased flexibility and created a more pleasant environment.

6. The Edinburgh University Library building is the largest university library in Great Brit-

ain. The *Brief* to the architects was based on research carried out by the librarian in both Britain and the United States of America, and it is a measure of his thoroughness that now, some 20 years later, the building still fulfills so well the demands of a modern academic library.[12] The building won the Royal Institute of British Architects (RIBA) Award in 1968, and the Civic Trust Award in 1969.

NOTTINGHAM UNIVERSITY LIBRARY

Faulkner-Brown was responsible for the architectural design of this particularly fine library. In accordance with his philosophy on academic library buildings, he reached agreement with the university on the qualities the library should possess, which would result in a building that was flexible, compact, accessible, extendible, varied, organized, comfortable, constant in environment, economic, and secure.[13] Some 16 years after completion, this impressive building still looks and feels relatively new and up-to-date. It is an example of Faulkner-Brown's vision, and

Architects:	Faulkner-Brown, Hendy, Watkinson, Stonor (Newcastle-upon-Tyne)
Size:	Total floor area—10,035 m² (108,000 ft²)
	Usable floor area—8,515 m² (92,000 ft²)
	Balance—1,520 m² (16,000 ft²)
	(17.85% of usable space)
Accommodation:	Book capacity—542,000
	Reader stations—1,200
	carrels—436
	tables—493
	easy chairs—151
	seminar—80
	studies—40
Costs:	Net cost—£805,975
	Furniture/fittings—£190,000
	Total cost—£995,975
	Cost/m²—£80.32
Completed:	August 1972
Librarian:	R. S. Smith

proof that the philosophy of this excellent architect, if adhered to as closely as possible, will produce a library that is an asset to any university campus.

SITE AND ACCESS

The university is located on a hill on the outskirts of Nottingham, and the site for the library determined by the university in July 1969 is well chosen (see Fig. 4.7). Savidge describes the building as being "positioned centrally on the tree-filled skyline of the Campus, its simple form clearly visible from the ring road and approach from the City. The panoramic view of the City adds much architectural interest," although it is not particularly attractive, dominated as it is by factories, terrace houses, and the Ratcliffe Power Station. The Library building is a dignified addition to the scene: "Its cleanly detailed concrete panels and dark, vertical slit windows enclosing restrained and well-proportioned spaces are a cool contrast to the miscellany of architectural styles which spread down the south-eastern slopes of the University site."[14] Set at the highest point of the campus, the library stands between the Faculty of Social Sciences and the School of Education, and is close to the Faculty of Arts. In addition, it is en route between halls of residence and the center of the university. Beautiful trees exist on the site, and the library has been positioned so as not to disrupt them. The building has enhanced the heart of the campus by providing a natural meeting point at the focus of established pedestrian routes. An added advantage is the slight slope of the ground, which has enabled the main entrance to be situated naturally on level two, and the service entrance on level one, with vehicular access. The loss of the central open space now occupied by the library may be regretted by some,[15] but the choice of site was clearly correct. As Metcalf[16] has stated: "It is a better site than is generally available for a new library in an old university."

EXTENDIBILITY

As may be seen from the site plan (Fig. 4.7), the location of the library to the south of the site achieves two purposes. First, it preserves the staff club and its beautiful surroundings without any overcrowding, at least for the foreseeable future. Second, it allows lateral extension of the library to the north, avoiding disruption of the existing pattern of trees. The precast panels of the north wall are designed so that they may be

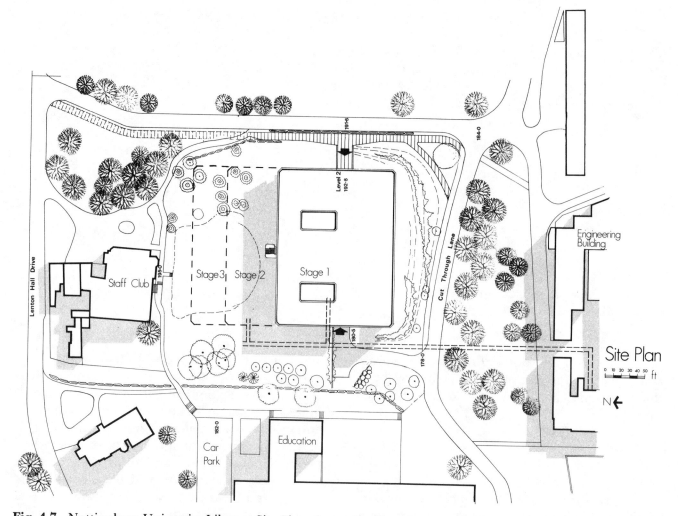

Fig. 4.7. Nottingham University Library: Site Plan. *Source:* FaulknerBrowns, Architects (Newcastle upon Tyne). "Nottingham University Library" (n.d.), p. 3. By permission from E.C. Watkinson of FaulknerBrowns.

removed from the façade and reused in the extended building.[17] There is, however, little likelihood of stages two and three (as indicated in Fig. 4.7) reaching completion, due to the restrictions placed on the size of university libraries by the University Grants Committee.

FLEXIBILITY

The library is on four levels, with the main floor at level two and the users' entrance on the east side. The delivery and service entrance is on level one, on the west of the building. Flexibility is of necessity reduced on level one, where plant rooms are located, and where the rare book

store and fumigation room require isolated environments. The three upper floors are completely open plan except for the two core areas containing lifts, stairs, toilets, and ducts.

Level one is a model of practical planning (see Fig. 4.8). It houses the manuscripts department, special collections, audiovisual room, photographic unit, fumigation room for the treatment of donations, a very useful general storage area, and a closed access storage stack with high shelving and good lighting. There is also a conference room, packing and delivery room, and binding preparation area.

At level two (Fig. 4.9), the principal elements of the library may be clearly seen from the entrance: the catalogues, reference and bibliogra-

Fig. 4.8. Nottingham University Library: Floor Plan, Level 1. *Source:* FaulknerBrowns, Architects (Newcastle upon Tyne). "Nottingham University Library" (n.d.), p. 3. By permission from E.C. Watkinson of FaulknerBrowns.

phy area, issue desk, the main stairs, the short loan collection, and facilities for recreation in the form of a coffee bar and smoking area. The foyer is large, with the issue desk set back to allow easy movement of traffic. Metcalf[18] has questioned the placing of this desk 30 m (98 ft) from the main entrance, and this is a valid point. Despite the spaciousness of the entrance foyer, readers borrowing books from the upper levels must walk some distance from the stairs to have them issued, and then retrace their steps to reach the exit control. Had the desk been closer to the exit, traffic patterns would have been simplified and fewer staff could have dealt with circulation, reserve books, and exit control (see Fig. 4.11). Behind the issue desk are the technical processing departments, a staff rest room and a machine room. Only the librarian and the depu-

ty librarian have separate offices. All other staff areas are open plan divided by shelving, the intention being that staff are accessible to users and that security of collections is discreetly increased. However, the staff areas appear to be overcrowded and are inadequately signposted.

Above the main floor are two levels of open-access bookstack and reading areas, one primarily for arts and the other for social sciences and government publications. Each level has space for approximately 187,000 books and 480 readers. Much care has been taken to provide a variety of reading environments. On these two floors open study carrels are located around the perimeter of the building, with tables nearby, and casual seating in the corner areas. Seminar rooms have been placed near the center of each floor, and hence have no outside windows. To

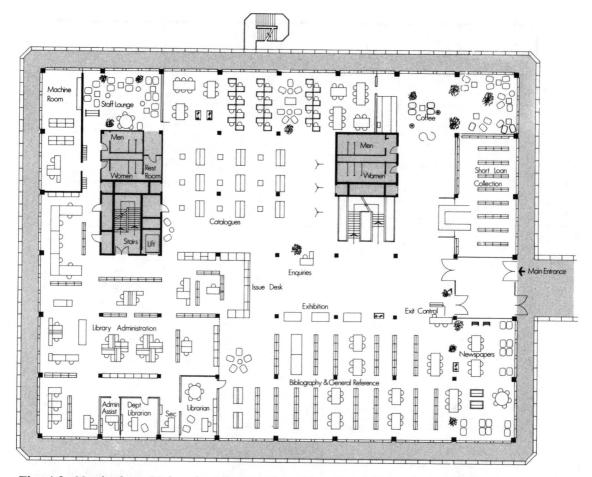

Fig. 4.9. Nottingham University Library: Floor Plan, Level 2. *Source:* FaulknerBrowns, Architects (Newcastle upon Tyne). "Nottingham University Library" (n.d.), p. 3. By permission from E.C. Watkinson of FaulknerBrowns.

overcome this, Faulkner-Brown has constructed one wall completely of glass, and this provides a view onto spaced bookstacks with windows beyond, thus successfully creating an impression of light and air not normally found in an inner room. The glazing was no more expensive than paneling, and curtains are provided should privacy be required.

With permanent walls reduced to a minimum, planning arrangements are extremely flexible. In his assessment of Nottingham University Library Metcalf[19] states:

> One of the important factors in a functional library building if the long-term view is taken is its flexibility. The University of Nottingham building is modular and is as flexible as a library building can be without adding unduly to its

cost. As services demand change, as they are almost sure to do during its lifetime, shifts of equipment and space assignments can be made with comparatively little difficulty or expense. It is doubtful if this requirement has been carried out more successfully anywhere in the United Kingdom.

INTERNAL ENVIRONMENT

The two upper floors of the library have been enclosed by heavy masonry walls, relieved by dark, vertical slit windows, spaced to give an economic arrangement of open carrels at the perimeter.[20] An unusual external feature is the glazed cutoff on each corner of the upper levels which adds character to the building externally and in-

Fig. 4.10. Nottingham University Library: View of Exterior. By permission from Peter Hoare, University Librarian.

Fig. 4.11. Nottingham University Library: View of Issue Desk. By permission from Peter Hoare, University Librarian.

ternally provides attractive informal study areas. In contrast, the main floor is almost totally glazed. It is shaded by the overhang of the upper levels, and heat retention is further reduced by the use of brown tinted glass. The lowest level is obscured somewhat by the slope of the ground, but is also primarily glass. Although the large amount of glass on level two takes into account the beautiful setting and also advertises the library within, the cantilevered overhang of 5.5 m (18 ft) reduces the area on this level by almost 500 m² (5,380 ft²).[21] Had this been available it might have made possible a reduction in the depth of the building and thus saved on construction costs. However, had there been no overhang, some form of screening would have been necessary to exclude heat and glare, and certainly some of the beauty of the building would have been lost by its reversion to a standard rectangular shape.

To maintain a comfortable internal environment in this deep, cubic building, constant, even illumination and humidity and temperature con-trol are essential. The skillful integration of heating, ventilation, and lighting has led to an ingenious ceiling solution, illustrated in Fig. 4.11. The wasted "dead" space above the usual flat suspended ceiling has been used to form sculpted panels, fitted between the structure and services.[22] Lighting is contained within these panels, and the coffered pattern gives a good level of illumination at the work surface (35 lumens) and in the bookstacks. The arrangement prevents glare, so that louvers on the fluo-rescent tubes are unnecessary, and in addition, the tubes consume a relatively small amount of power. The coffered pattern gives additional height and volume to the reading and book areas, adding to the comfort of the user. It also has a greater sound-absorbent effect than the conventional ceiling.

Air conditioning provides reasonably com-fortable working conditions. However, system failures have caused serious problems on occa-sion as there are no opening windows in the building.

Fig. 4.12 Nottingham University Library: View of Reference Area, Level 2. By permission from Peter Hoare, University Librarian.

As regards power, the ground floor has cable conduiting on a grid basis, which allows total flexibility. Other levels have power points on the external walls, pillars, and central core areas.

The furniture in the library was custom-made, and generally designed to provide a wide variety of reading environments. It is strong, attractive, and relatively maintenance-free, and its quality seems to have dissuaded users from abusing it.[23] Reading areas are comfortable, and indoor plants have been used very successfully in the creation of a congenial atmosphere. Although there is good provision for undisturbed study in quiet and isolated surroundings, the obvious popularity of the main floor reference tables and casual areas (see Fig. 4.12), as well as the informal seating by the large corner windows on levels three and four, bring to question the provision of substantial numbers of individual study carrels (436). It would seem that many students enjoy and prefer the environment of the open areas and find the hum of background activity an aid to concentration. There is, however, a wide choice of reader stations providing for individual preferences.

ECONOMY

The architect has produced a deep, rectangular, four-story building 59 m long, 46 m wide, and 16 m high (193′ 6″ × 159′ × 52′ 6″), with a low wall : floor ratio of 0.4 : 1.0. Thus the cost of external walling is contained, but the need for a constant environment tends to transfer cost from exterior elements to ventilation and electrical services. The suspended trough ceiling is economic in that it serves three functions: "It forms a flexible service distribution zone, gives a measure of concealment to the bare fluorescent tubes, and provides for sound absorption. Further acoustic treatment is provided by carpeting on the upper levels."[24]

Nottingham University Library has a feeling

Fig. 4.13. Nottingham University Library: Passage Area on Level 1 Illustrating Maintenance-Free Surfaces. By permission from Peter Hoare, University Librarian.

of luxury about it, even though it was built within the UGC's financial limits and has been in existence for many years. A factor contributing to this is the easy maintenance finishes used throughout the building. On the lower level the internal walls are of brick, and the floor is of white linoleum tiles which have remained bright and clean (see Fig. 4.13). On the upper levels no plaster or paint is used on the walls. Surfaces are either glass, teak paneling, or brick. The carpeting is of good quality and has worn well.

ASSESSMENT

Hoare,[25] present university librarian, has stated:

> After many years of heavy use the building's design has been well justified. Some modification to layout has been made, but owing to the open plan layout on Levels Two, Three and Four, this has been easy. Open plan work areas seem to have been accepted by the library staff, but provision for private consultation with readers sometimes seems a little inadequate. Total reliance on a mechanical ventilation system has led to difficulties when chilling or (less often) heating equipment has not operated properly. Readers find it an exceptionally good place to work. The design, high quality of finishes and

easy maintenance undoubtedly contribute much to the Library's popularity and good reputation in the University.

From an aesthetic point of view, Nottingham University Library takes advantage of an attractive natural environment. It is very pure in concept and is a good example of open plan design. It has many satisfactory features found only too rarely in university libraries. The lighting is attractive and of good quality. The closed access bookstack on the first level is cost-effective and convenient. The planning of space on this level is very satisfactory, and the fact that much of it is below ground level is countered by the fact that library staff and readers are provided with windows and some natural light, while storage areas occupy the inner spaces.[26] The public areas are attractive and well planned, and the variety and quality of seating provided for readers are very successful. The close collaboration of librarian and architect is evident throughout the building. The impression one gains is of spaciousness and efficiency, coupled with immaculate detailing and workmanship, proving that a good architect can combine excellent design with economy. Nottingham University Library remains one of the finest examples of British library architecture.

LOUGHBOROUGH UNIVERSITY OF TECHNOLOGY LIBRARY

Architects: Faulkner-Brown, Hendy, Watkinson, Stonor (Newcastle-upon-Tyne)
Size: Gross area—9,263 m² (99,700 ft²)
Library—6,554 m² (70,500 ft²)
Department—900 m² (9,700 ft²)
Balance—1,809 m² (19,500 ft²) (24% of usable)
Capacity: 600,000 volumes
Reader stations: 800
Costs: Building—£2,500,000
Furniture/shelving—£600,000
Total—£3,100,000
Cost/m²—£270
Opened: September 1980
Librarian: A. J. Evans

In 1976 the University Grants Committee authorized the building of a new library at the Loughborough University of Technology. Work began in March 1978, and the library opened its doors in September 1980. The building, which is named after the university's first chancellor, Lord Pilkington, houses the library on levels one, two, and three, and the Department of Library and Information Studies on level four. It is planned according to the concept of the "teaching library," and there are common facilities and accommodations for both the university library and the department. Evans,[27] the university librarian, has outlined the reasons for a shared building:

1. In terms of educational advantage, students will be in the environment of a vigorous library service, and may participate in many aspects of the Library's work without impairing its efficiency;
2. Library staff will have the benefit of the expertise and professional interest of the Department, and Departmental staff and students can maintain close contact with the practical work situation;
3. It is convenient for the Department to be close to the Library collection;
4. Many common needs may be met by shared accommodation and equipment, thus maintaining economical use of resources:

   - shared seminar/teaching facilities;
   - increased bibliographical coverage and no wasteful duplication in a departmental collection;
   - shared use of expensive equipment, e.g. computer terminals;
   - shared staffroom and services.

The library has been planned to provide for a university population of 5,500 students and 800 academic and research staff. It will provide for growth of the present collection of approximately 380,000 to 600,000 volumes, with storage provision for 100,000 volumes elsewhere on campus.[28] Although the space allocation was based entirely on UGC norms, these have proved to be adequate at Loughborough where the existing stock is still relatively small.

THE BRIEF

The university specified a very adaptable building with a flexible layout and the possibility of expansion should this become necessary. The library was to be inviting and functional rather than impressive, with an atmosphere in all public areas that was appropriate for study without the need for oppressive silence. There was to be variety in the provision of reader stations, the layout such that users could easily identify their position, and all traffic in and out of the library controlled from one point close to the entrance.[29]

The firm of Faulkner-Brown, Hendy, Watkinson, and Stonor was appointed on the strength of Faulkner-Brown's achievements at the universities of Nottingham, Cardiff, and St. Andrews. In terms of the university's requirements for flexibility, comfort, and convenience, it was an excellent choice. Faulkner-Brown has designed an attractive, comfortable, open plan library that is well used. He has applied his "ten desirable qualities" to the design and layout of this building, although possibly to a slightly lesser degree than is the case at Nottingham University Library, and the result is a functional and efficient building.

SITE

The campus of the Loughborough University of Technology is widespread, and on first impression it is difficult to discern the center and focal point of traffic and student movement. However, the library is in close proximity to a number of teaching blocks and the refectory, and is well served by pedestrian pathways, roads, and a large parking area (see Fig. 4.14). With a restriction on the height of the building imposed by the university planners,[30] the architect has sunk the library into a hole dug from the campus hillside, the natural slope of the ground reducing the amount of excavation necessary. The landscaping of the surrounding area is particularly successful.

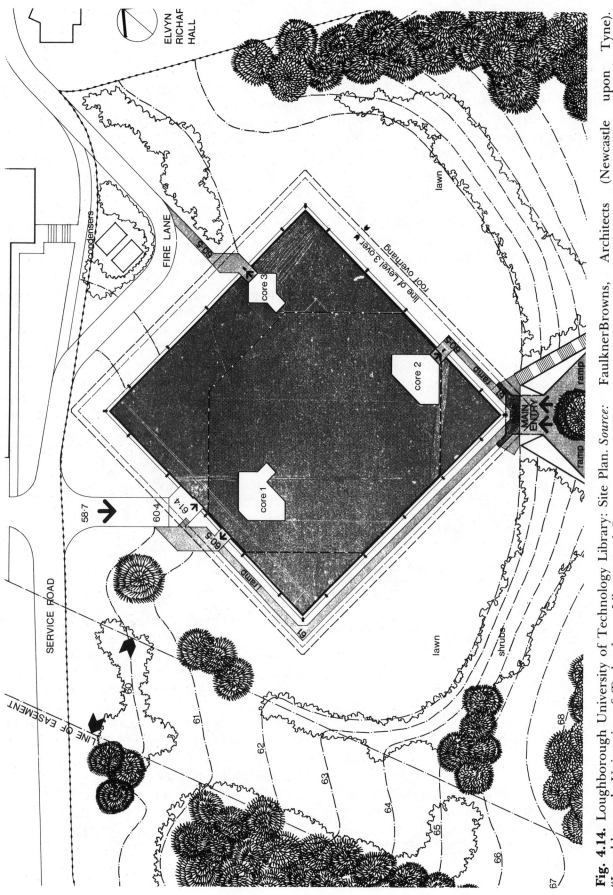

Fig. 4.14. Loughborough University of Technology Library: Site Plan. *Source:* FaulknerBrowns, Architects (Newcastle upon Tyne). "Loughborough University of Technology: Library and Department of Library and Information Studies" (n.d.). By permission from E.C. Watkinson of FaulknerBrowns.

FLEXIBILITY

As in many libraries, level one is less flexible than the other levels because of the necessity for locating machinery as well as delivery and loading areas at this level. As indicated on the floor plan (Fig. 4.15), much space is permanently taken up by plantroom, air conditioning equipment, loading dock, binding preparation area, and closed access stack. There are a number of solid walls in this area to isolate machinery and reduce noise. The remainder of level one is entirely open plan and houses the university's main book and periodical collections in science and technology. User core areas are on the north and east sides of the building, that on the east being the major access point containing stairs, lift, toilets, and emergency exit. There is an information desk situated close by. This is a very practical arrangement. The "noise" area is contained at the center of movement, leaving the rest of the library relatively quiet, and students requiring assistance may find it immediately on entering each level. The core on the west side is for staff use only.

An interesting feature of the Pilkington Library is its diagonal arrangement. Although square in shape, internal design emphasizes the diagonal, adding interest to the layout and creating attractive reader areas. The wall separating machinery from stack and reading space on this first level runs from northeast to southwest, and the bookstacks run from the center toward the periphery at right angles to this line. A number of soundproof study carrels and a seminar room are provided in the inner areas, while remaining study stations are situated on the periphery. The atmosphere is a little oppressive in the inner areas on this level, possibly due to the existence of the dividing partition which blocks the view to the north and west. The architect has done his best to make this inner area as attractive as possible by avoiding a long, straight wall. He has created interesting shapes, within which are groups of casual chairs and tables.

Level two is more flexible in that the only permanent features are the three user cores (see Fig. 4.16). Surrounding these are soundproof study carrels, seminar rooms, and on the east, an

information desk. This level contains the main book and periodical collections in the arts, humanities, and social sciences. Reader stations are located around the perimeter and in the central area between the two banks of bookstacks.

Level three is the entrance level on which most library services are located, including the issue, short loan and interlibrary loan desks, and reference, current periodicals, audiovisual, and microform collections (see Fig. 4.17). Also on this level are staff areas such as technical processing and administration. Apart from the core areas all walls are demountable to maintain flexibility. Air brick partitions separate staff from public areas.

Level four is much smaller than the three main levels of the library, and is set in from the external walls of the building. It is thus barely visible from ground level, in accordance with the height restriction on all buildings on the campus. Here is housed the university's Department of Library and Information Studies. The shape of the department is octagonal, with staff and administrative offices situated around the perimeter, accessible via an internal corridor. The inner spaces are occupied by stack, laboratory, and teaching areas. This section is less flexible than the other levels of the library, but as it is a teaching department and is unlikely to be used for any other purpose, flexibility is not such an important factor.

The ducting on all levels is visible and of unpainted aluminum. Apart from providing flexibility, this method is the most economical way of meeting the strict fire regulations in the United Kingdom.[31] Were the ducting to be contained within a false ceiling, expensive fireproof partitioning would be required at frequent intervals.

COMPACTNESS

Faulkner-Brown has created an almost ideal building in terms of this quality. Its inverted pyramid shape is nearly as compact as the recommended cube. Level one is 50 m (164 ft) square increasing via level two to level three which is 60 m square (197 ft square). It functions very efficiently in that travel distances for readers, staff,

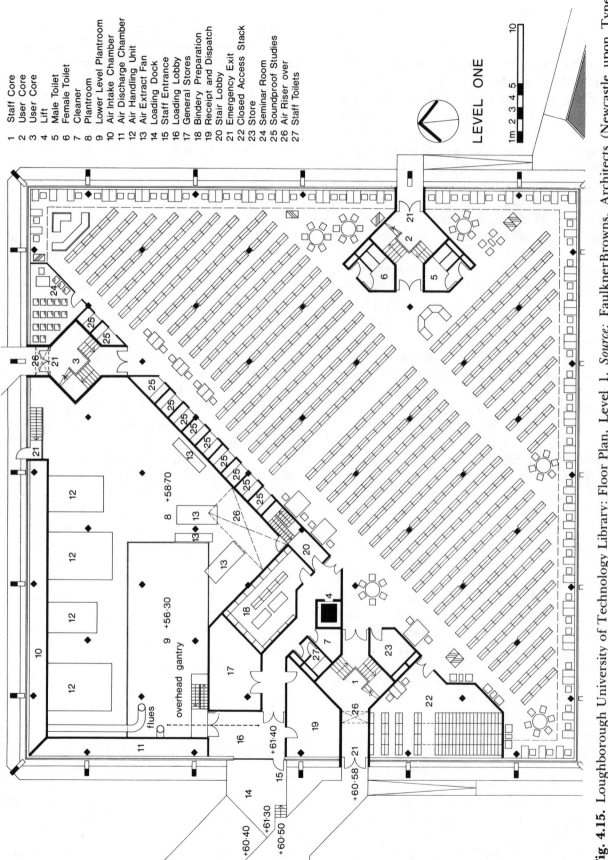

1 Staff Core
2 User Core
3 User Core
4 Lift
5 Male Toilet
6 Female Toilet
7 Cleaner
8 Plantroom
9 Lower Level Plantroom
10 Air Intake Chamber
11 Air Discharge Chamber
12 Air Handling Unit
13 Air Extract Fan
14 Loading Dock
15 Staff Entrance
16 Loading Lobby
17 General Stores
18 Bindery Preparation
19 Receipt and Dispatch
20 Stair Lobby
21 Emergency Exit
22 Closed Access Stack
23 Store
24 Seminar Room
25 Soundproof Studies
26 Air Riser over
27 Staff Toilets

LEVEL ONE

1m 2 3 4 5   10

Fig. 4.15. Loughborough University of Technology Library: Floor Plan, Level 1. *Source:* FaulknerBrowns, Architects (Newcastle upon Tyne). "Loughborough University of Technology: Library and Department of Library and Information Studies" (n.d.). By permission from E.C. Watkinson of FaulknerBrowns.

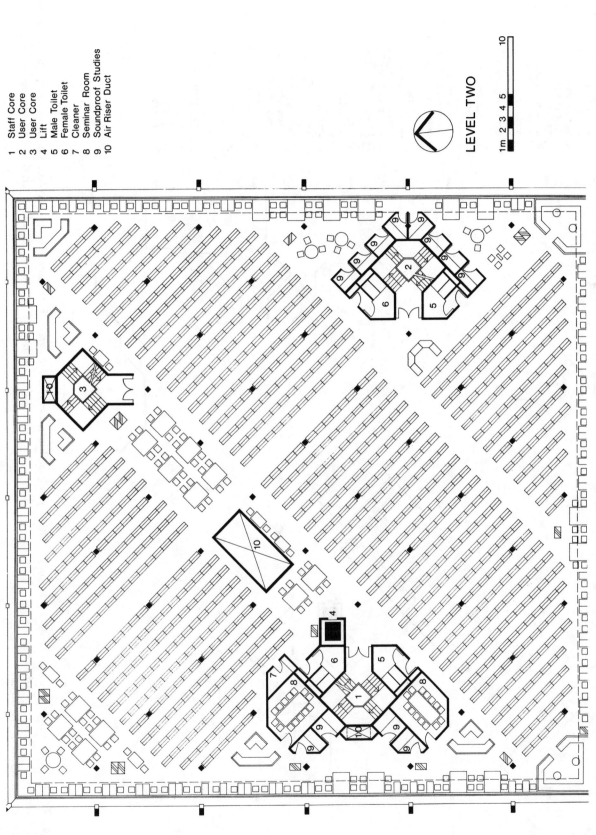

1 Staff Core
2 User Core
3 User Corce
4 Lift
5 Male Toilet
6 Female Toilet
7 Cleaner
8 Seminar Room
9 Soundproof Studies
10 Air Riser Duct

LEVEL TWO

1m 2 3 4 5   10

Fig. 4.16. Loughborough University of Technology Library: Floor Plan, Level 2. *Source:* FaulknerBrowns, Architects (Newcastle upon Tyne). "Loughborough University of Technology: Library and Department of Library and Information Studies" (n.d.). By permission from E.C. Watkinson of FaulknerBrowns.

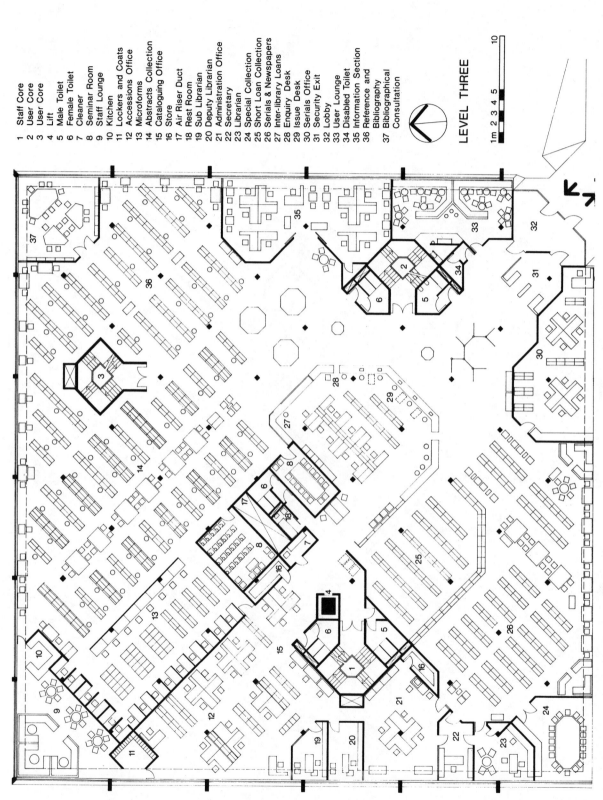

1 Staff Core
2 User Core
3 User Core
4 Lift
5 Male Toilet
6 Female Toilet
7 Cleaner
8 Seminar Room
9 Staff Lounge
10 Kitchen
11 Lockers and Coats
12 Accessions Office
13 Microforms
14 Abstracts Collection
15 Cataloguing Office
16 Store
17 Air Riser Duct
18 Rest Room
19 Sub Librarian
20 Deputy Librarian
21 Administration Office
22 Secretary
23 Librarian
24 Special Collection
25 Short Loan Collection
26 Serials & Newspapers
27 Inter-library Loans
28 Enquiry Desk
29 Issue Desk
30 Serials Office
31 Security Exit
32 Lobby
33 User Lounge
34 Disabled Toilet
35 Information Section
36 Reference and
   Bibliography
37 Bibliographical
   Consultation

LEVEL THREE

1m 2 3 4 5   10

Fig. 4.17. Loughborough University of Technology Library: Floor Plan, Level 3. *Source:* FaulknerBrowns, Architects (Newcastle upon Tyne). "Loughborough University of Technology: Library and Department of Library and Information Studies" (n.d.). By permission from E.C. Watkinson of FaulknerBrowns.

and books are kept to a minimum. Consumption of energy is also minimized.

ACCESSIBILITY

Accessibility is good, both from the exterior into the building and from the entrance to all parts of the building. The entrance is on level three, due to the siting of the library on a hillside. This entrance is unusual and has been the cause of some comment. A wide set of steps leads to large double doors, which, unlike most public buildings, are constructed of solid dark wood. More reminiscent of an English manor house than a modern library, they are pleasingly different. On entering, one finds a small, attractive lobby, decorated with colorful pot plants. A second set of doors, constructed of glass, leads into the library. Signposting is very clear at this initial point of entry.

The main desk is set back from the entrance. One might question this in terms of security, but one cannot deny that it occupies a focal position on the main level, emphasized by a lowered ceil-

ing over the area. Various library services are located in close proximity to the main desk, and it is well placed in terms of traffic routes and the main stairs. Accessibility within the building is enhanced by the siting of user cores in the same place on each level, by the provision of information desks at these points, and by exceptionally good signposting throughout. The latter includes:

- signs hanging from the ceiling to indicate the bookstacks;
- floor plans on each level;
- large signs at the entrance and in the stairwells;
- printed guides to various aspects of the library and its services available at all information desks.

The library is organized so that most materials are visible, accessible, and easily available. On levels one and two in particular, the layout is very simple. As far as the users are concerned, they will very soon become familiar with the library. Level three, because of the variety of ser-

Fig. 4.18. Loughborough University of Technology Library: View of Exterior

Fig. 4.19. Loughborough University of Technology Library: View of Exterior, Southeast Corner

vices offered, is naturally more complex. However, the fact that unfamiliar users on entering the library are brought immediately to the focal point—the issue and inquiry desk—ensures that they are quickly directed to the relevant section.

VARIETY

Loughborough, like many university libraries, has moved away from the concept of large reading rooms and instead reader stations have, where possible, been located around the perimeter of the library.[32] This provides the user with a pleasant outlook and natural light. A variety of study tables for one, two, or four persons, together with open study carrels, lockable carrels,

seminar rooms, and informal seating permit users to select the type of seating and level of privacy most suited to their needs. Enhancing this variety of study areas is a bright and colorful choice of internal finishes (see Fig. 4.20). The carpeting is russet in color throughout the library. Internal joinery and furniture is of light oak and beechwood, the most impressive example being the issue desk. Shelving is metal, of a light mushroom color, with beechwood end panels. These are matched in the reference and bibliographic collections by specially fitted beech desk plates, to facilitate ease of use of this material (see Fig. 4.21). Contrasting with the pale wood and shelving is the bright red and green upholstery of the chairs. The visual impact of the interior is largely determined by these contrasts, and further enhanced by the generous use of well-stocked plant containers throughout the building.

COMFORT

The library is fully air conditioned, with temperature and humidity levels controlled at an acceptable and comfortable level. The floors are carpeted, providing a large degree of acoustic absorption in the large, open plan areas. Staff work areas and those containing machinery are partitioned off from the public areas of the library, thus further lowering the noise level.

Of interest is the lighting, which consists of fluorescent tubes arranged in an arrow-head pattern, running at right angles to the bookstacks. This ensures a good level of illumination at the work surface, and also permits adequate light to reach the lowest level of the bookstacks. Large windows around the perimeter of the building permit much natural light to enter and make the peripheral areas particularly attractive to the user.

SECURITY

The need for security has been kept in mind in the design of this library. All movement in and out of the building is channeled through one entrance/exit point protected by an electronic

Fig. 4.20. Loughborough University of Technology Library: Study Area

book detection system and which, although some distance away, is in full view of staff at the issue desk. Open plan permits a certain amount of staff control, although this is somewhat reduced on levels one and two by the angle of the book-stacks. There are emergency exits on three sides of the building.

EXTERNAL FEATURES

The structure of the Pilkington Library consists of reinforced concrete floors and columns on a 6.6 m (21′ 8″) grid, with raking columns at the perimeter supporting the overhanging floors and providing much of the character of the building (see Fig. 4.19). Lateral stability is provided by the stairs and lift cores. The main floor is level with the street, and is the largest. This floor overhangs the floor below to provide shading, and similarly with the level below that. External columns are fairfaced concrete, and spandrels and fascias white profiled aluminum sheet. The top floor is glazed in gray antisun glass fixed into a black anodized aluminum framework.[33]

ASSESSMENT

In all, this Faulkner-Brown library is further proof of the architect's talent. It is well planned, functional, and contains many of the qualities needed in a university library. It is flexible. It is inviting and practical rather than impressive. The atmosphere in public areas is appropriate to study yet bright and cheerful. A wide variety of study spaces is provided, and signage is excellent. It is in fact difficult to fault this library in any major way. Possible minor flaws are:

- One of the support columns on the exterior of the building partially blocks one of the emergency exits.[34]
- As is the case with Nottingham University Library, the issue desk is some distance from the entrance, reducing security and staff control. Its location also requires users emerging from the main stairwell to walk back to the desk before leaving the library if they require books to be issued.
- The lobby is small, and at busy times some congestion could result.

Fig. 4.21. Loughborough University of Technology Library: Shelving in the Reference Area

Despite these points, the Loughborough University of Technology has a library that works, one in which the students feel comfortable. Internally it combines warmth with practicality, while externally it is perhaps the most attractive building on the campus.

REFERENCES

EDINBURGH UNIVERSITY LIBRARY

1. Edinburgh University Library, *"Notes for Visitors,"* rev. ed. (Edinburgh: University Library, 1982), p.3.
2. "Library at University of Edinburgh," *Architects' Journal,* Information Library, June 1968 (SFB 97), p.1392.
3. Edinburgh University, *"Brief for New Main Library Building,"* 1961–1962, p.ii (unpublished).
4. Ibid.
5. "Five university libraries," *Architects' Journal,* Information Library, March 1968 (SFB 97), p.575.
6. Edinburgh University, p.i.
7. Personal communication from I.D. Thomson, Librarian (Building and Planning) at University of Edinburgh Library, July 1983.
8. Edinburgh University, p.3.
9. "Library at University of Edinburgh," p.1394.
10. "Five university libraries," p.570.
11. "Library at University of Edinburgh," p.1400.
12. Ibid., p.1394.

NOTTINGHAM UNIVERSITY LIBRARY

13. Faulkner-Brown, Hendy, Watkinson, and Stonor (architects), *Nottingham University Library* (Newcastle-upon-Tyne, n.d.), p.2.
14. R. Savidge, "Nottingham University Library: an architect's outlook," *Architects' Journal,* 24 April, 1974, p.900.
15. Ibid.
16. K.D. Metcalf, "Nottingham University Library: appraisal from a librarian's point of view," *Architects' Journal,* 24 April, 1974, p.901.
17. "Nottingham University Library," *Architects' Journal,* 24 April, 1974, p.899.
18. Metcalf, p.905.
19. Ibid., p.901.
20. "Nottingham University Library," p.899.
21. Metcalf, p.902.
22. *New Library Buildings,* ed. H. Ward (London: Library Association, 1976), p.245.
23. Personal communication from P. Hoare, university librarian, to delegates on the British Council Course on Library Planning and Design. London and Birmingham, October 1981.
24. "Nottingham University Library: cost comment," *Architects' Journal,* 24 April, 1974, p.910.
25. Personal communication from P. Hoare.
26. Metcalf, p.907.

LOUGHBOROUGH UNIVERSITY OF TECHNOLOGY LIBRARY

27. A.J. Evans and A.F. MacDougall, "The planning of the new Loughborough University Library and Department of Library and Information Studies," *International Association of Technological University Libraries,* Proceedings, vol. 11, 1979, p.19.

28. Ibid., p.20.
29. Ibid., p.24.
30. Personal communication from Godfrey Thompson, city librarian, London (at the time), and planning consultant, with whom I visited this library in 1982.

31. Ibid.
32. Evans, p.23.
33. "Library, Loughborough University," *Architectural Review,* vol.163, no.971, January 1974, p.54.
34. Pointed out to me by Godfrey Thompson when we visited this library.

5 United States of America: Case Studies

UNIVERSITY OF NORTHERN IOWA LIBRARY

Architects:	Thorson, Brom, Broshar, and Snyder (Waterloo, Iowa)
Interior design:	Westburg, Klaus Associates (Minneapolis, Minnesota)
Librarian:	D.O. Rod
Total floor area:	16,275 m² (175,200 ft²)
Shelving capacity:	700,000 volumes
Reader stations:	1,550
Facilities:	11 student group studies
	23 faculty studies
	7 general lounges
	3 smoking lounges
	2 typing rooms
Total cost:	$4,450,000
Cost/m²:	$273 (including fittings)
Occupation date:	Unit 1—September 1964
	Unit 2—January 1975

SITE

The University of Northern Iowa is located in spacious grounds on the outskirts of Cedar Falls, Iowa. The library is situated in the center of the campus with the student union to the east, the campanile to the west, and academic buildings to the north and south. Student residences are on the perimeter of the campus. The site of the library is ideal for projected development of the university. At present orientation is toward the east, with the main entrance in close proximity to the union (see Fig. 5.1). Accessibility is good from all points on the campus.

The University of Northern Iowa Library, like many other academic libraries, has occupied numerous locations on the campus since its incep-

tion in 1876. In 1964 unit 1 of the present library building was occupied—8,668 m² (93,300 ft²), 275,000 volumes, 1,100 reader stations. Unit 2, completed in 1975, is designed to accommodate present and continuing needs—16,275 m² (175,200 ft²), 700,000 volumes, 1,550 reader stations. Both units were built at times of recession and hence the bids tendered were low. A high-quality building is the result.

BRIEF

Donald O. Rod, librarian at the University of Northern Iowa and consultant on numerous building projects in the United States, listed the

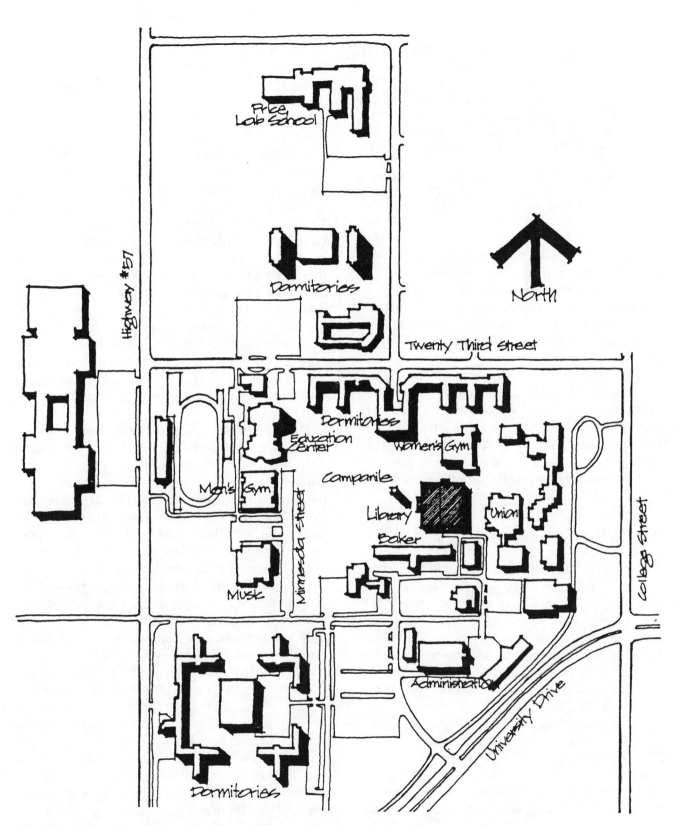

Fig. 5.1. University of Northern Iowa Library: Site Plan. *Source:* Thorson-Brom-Broshar-Snyder, Architects (Waterloo, Iowa). "University of Northern Iowa Library Master Plan" (1971), p. 4. By permission from Barbara Jones, Director of Library Services, University of Northern Iowa.

four major concerns of the library in his *Brief*[1] to the architects:

- supporting the instructional and research programs of the institution;
- aiding the faculty (within budgetary limitations) in their research and other scholarly activities;
- encouraging students to acquire and develop lifetime learning skills and habits;
- participating in reciprocal service with the larger community, both state and national.

The *Brief* was a comprehensive document providing the architects with detailed information on requirements, collections, spatial relationships, major elements, and circulation statistics. Tables of growth over 10 years were also provided (estimated at 8% compounded annually).

The overall success of the first unit was a major design constraint on the architects. The *Brief* stated that the very satisfactory module size should be continued in the expansion, and that the functional layout of the initial structure worked so well that the same basic arrangement and pattern of relationships should be retained.[2]

EXTENDIBILITY

The original 1964 structure was built so that extension could take place both horizontally and vertically. In order to retain the necessary services on the main level of the building and to preserve good functional relationships among these services, initial expansion was horizontal to the west with the addition of a unit almost the same size as the existing structure. Future expansion will be vertical.

Throughout the building the staircases and lounge areas have a live load capacity of 4.79 kN/m^2 (98 lbs/ft^2), while all general floor areas as well as the existing roof have a capacity of 6 kN/m^2 (125 lbs/ft^2). Although the first unit is able to carry only one additional floor, unit 2 has footing and columns of sufficient strength to support several additional floors. These would ultimately be built to contain lesser-used mate-

rial, and construction of a fourth level is envisaged in the early 1990s.

FLEXIBILITY

The original building was modular and highly flexible, with supporting columns 7.78 m (25' 6") apart, center on center, in both directions, thus leaving 7.32 m (24 ft) clear between columns. This module size has been continued in the 1975 extension. With columns under 450 mm (±18 ins) in diameter, it has been possible to bury them in walls and stack ranges, thus eliminating any sense of a maze of columns which could so easily have resulted. The present expanded library is on three levels with the main floor at level two (Figs. 5.2, 5.3, and 5.4 indicate the floor plans). The library is based on open plan design, and with the exception of core areas containing stairs, lifts, and toilets, all walls and partitions are demountable.

Much care has gone into the design of the major elements of this library. The main floor is outstanding in both its logical arrangement and ambience. The entrance lobby is spacious and inviting, with a large circulation desk area located immediately to the left on entering. Ahead of it is an attractive, informally furnished new book display area with wooden island shelving and bright carpeting and seating. It is tastefully decorated with small modern sculptures and indoor plants. Apart from breaking the monotony of a large lobby, this provides an inviting waiting area for patrons near the entrance. Wall space has been used for the display of paintings, pottery, and other art forms to give added attractiveness and function. To the right of the entrance is the main staircase, one of the highlights of the building. The architects wished to build a spiral staircase, but Rod disagreed from a safety point of view.[3] The result is a compromise; a beautiful elliptical stair with steps of even width and the stairwell finished in deep red glazed brick. The elliptical shape is emphasized by an artwork hanging in the stairwell—a magnificent woven tapestry in natural earth colors. The lobby of any library provides patrons with an initial

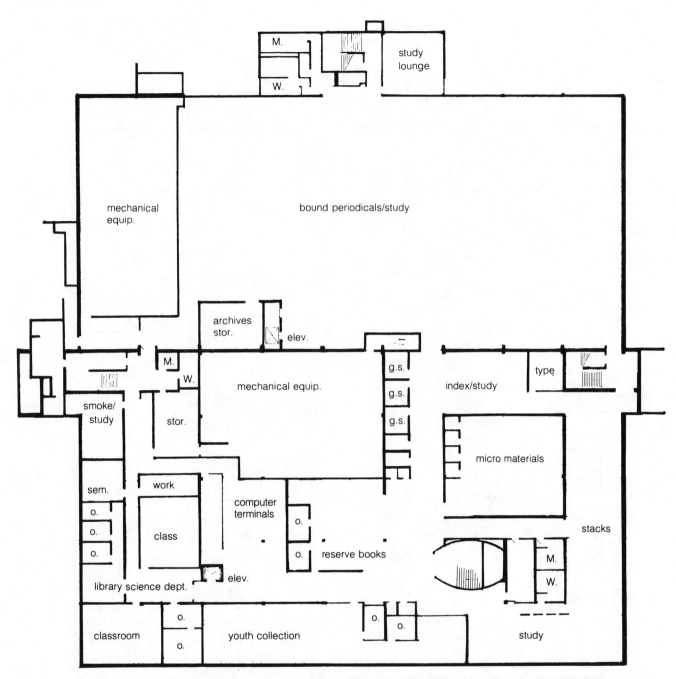

Fig. 5.2. University of Northern Iowa Library: Floor Plan, Level 1. *Source:* "Finding Your Way Around the UNI Library." Cedar Falls, Iowa: UNI Library, 1983. By permission from Barbara Jones, Director of Library Services, University of Northern Iowa.

impression; at the University of Northern Iowa Library this is overwhelmingly positive.

The administrative suite is located in the southeast corner of the building (see Fig. 5.3), and contains offices for the director and two assistant directors, a small conference room that can accommodate 12 people, a reception and general office area, storeroom, bookkeeping room, and staff lounge. The latter is easily accessible from both the administrative suite and the Technical Processing Department. The office of the assistant director (public relations)

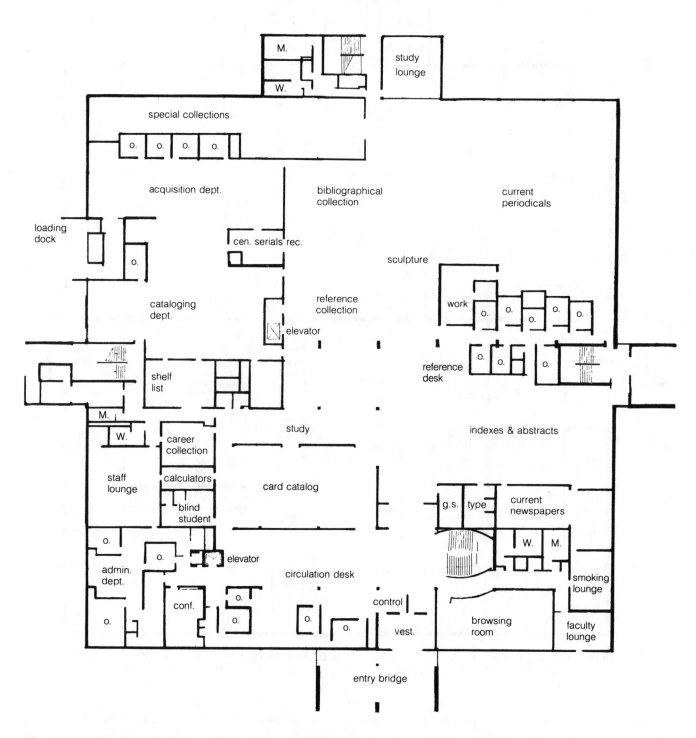

Fig. 5.3. University of Northern Iowa Library: Floor Plan, Level 2. *Source:* "Finding Your Way Around the UNI Library." Cedar Falls, Iowa: UNI Library, 1983. By permission from Barbara Jones, Director of Library Services, University of Northern Iowa.

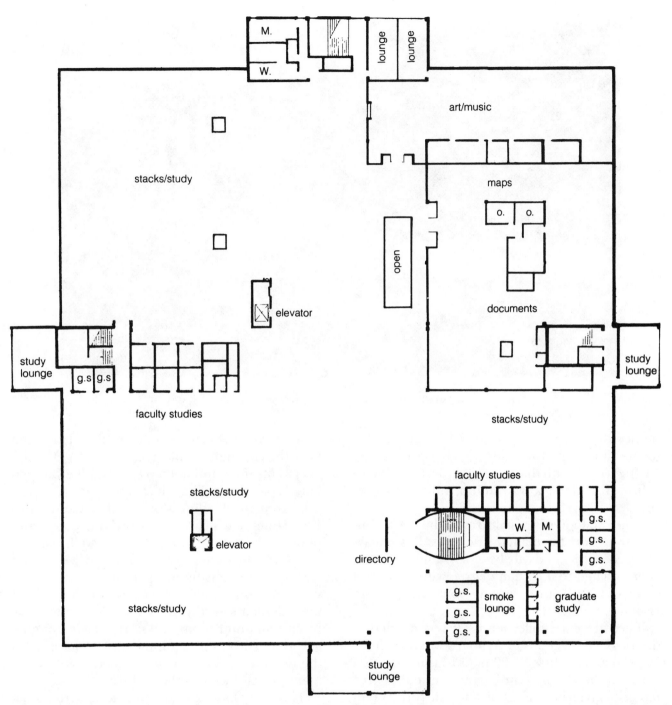

Fig. 5.4. University of Northern Iowa Library: Floor Plan, Level 3. *Source:* "Finding Your Way Around the UNI Library." Cedar Falls, Iowa: UNI Library, 1983. By permission from Barbara Jones, Director of Library Services, University of Northern Iowa.

and the conference room are directly accessible from the corridor outside the administrative suite.

The Readers' Services Department is the central information point of the library, consisting of a sizable core of reference librarians and support personnel surrounded by such major tools as the catalogue, reference and bibliographic collections, indexes, abstracts, current journals, newspapers, and micromaterials. The central

Fig. 5.5. University of Northern Iowa Library: View of Exterior

service desk of the department is clearly visible to the library patron immediately on entering. In the vicinity of the reference desk are eight offices for staff, a workroom, and a storage room.

The catalogue is visible from the lobby but removed from the main traffic lanes. It is a heavily used area, tends to be noisy, and thus has been isolated to a certain degree with acoustical glass partitions that confine sound yet retain visibility.

The reference collection itself is contained in double-faced sections of standard wooden shelving. An aisle width of 1.22 m (4 ft) is maintained between the ranges. The current periodical area has been given identification and control through skillful placing of shelving, yet it retains an inviting, informal character (see Fig. 5.6).

Also associated with the readers' services area are a room equipped for blind students and a room containing useful items such as staplers, calculators, guillotines, and punches. This tool room has proved immensely popular with students.[4]

On the southwest of this main level is the Tech-

nical Services Department, conveniently located near the catalogue, bibliographic center, and delivery entrance, and not too far from the Circulation Department. There is easy movement of parcels from the loading dock to the Acquisitions Department, which deals with both books and periodicals. The Mailing Room is well planned and very functional (see Fig. 5.7). Offices within Technical Processing are partially glazed to ensure a pleasant interior yet retain privacy. Further elements in this area include a stationery room, computer room, and storage room for gifts and minor items of equipment. Also located on the main level is the Special Collections Department, which includes the archives.

The first floor, on the lower level, provides a large area for stack and study, as well as several services. Reserve books are in the area immediately facing the main staircase. Computer terminals are located behind the reserve book area; these do not belong to the library but space is provided for their use by students. The youth collection, containing materials typically found in school libraries, is a long, narrow room on the east side. The Department of Library Science is

Fig. 5.6. University of Northern Iowa Library: Periodicals Reading Room

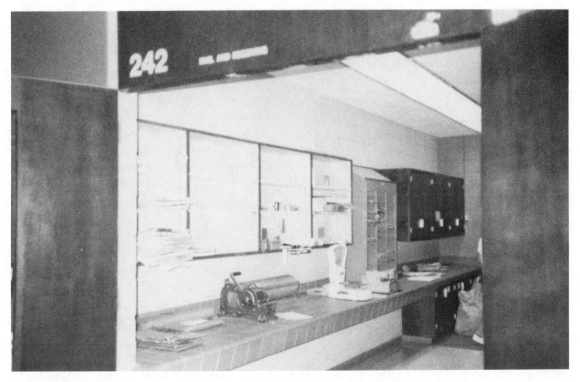

Fig. 5.7. University of Northern Iowa Library: Mailing Room

located in the southeast corner, and operates independently of the library.

The third floor, or upper level, is primarily stack and study space. However, two separate collections are housed on this level. Documents and maps are located on the north side. This is a large area with a service counter, two staff offices, and a workroom serving both collections which are contiguous but separately identified. The second is art and music, where the physical format of the materials and the need for specialized equipment for their use has necessitated separation from the general bookstock. There are two staff offices, a workroom, service counter, group listening rooms, and a number of informal reader stations. A network of conduits and raceways makes possible the connection of all listening stations to a central console behind the service desk.

Generally the library is well planned and very adaptable. In the stack areas aisle widths are 1.07 m (3 ft). Rod believes that wider aisles encourage more browsing and greater use of the library's stock. However, they take up space, and it is likely that they will have to be reduced in the near future. Fortunately this will not affect lighting too adversely. Only half the available lights are used at present, and the level of light could be raised if they were no longer centered on aisles. To cater for automation a false ceiling has been installed, allowing a space of 460 mm (18 ins) for cabling throughout the library.

INTERNAL ENVIRONMENT

The State of Iowa experiences extremes of climate in summer and winter, and much care has been given to the provision of a comfortable internal environment. The air conditioning system is on the whole very satisfactory, with rapid air change, absence of drafts, and quiet operation. Better humidity control and an improved exhaust system in the smoking lounges are possible areas for improvement.

The building contains narrow slit thermopane windows on the upper levels,[5] and a 1.22 m (4 ft) overhang to protect the large expanse of glass on the main level. On the west wall the architect has managed to take advantage of the fine views of the campus without introducing too much heat and glare in summer. The primary purpose of fenestration continues to be aesthetic and psychological, with the provision of natural light a secondary and relatively unimportant consideration. The polarized fluorescent lighting used in unit 1 was a very successful feature. However, it was thought that it would be desirable in nonwork areas to introduce other types of lighting to give subtle contrast to a building which would eventually be sizable. Lighting in the extension ranges from 70 foot-candles down to 40 in some areas. Small round incandescent lights are used in the central passageways and reference sections, and reading stations in the latter areas are very popular. Troffered recessed lights are used in large stack areas. An attempt has been made to create a variety of moods in a structure that is by its nature very orderly and controlled.

To retain the feeling of spaciousness, the ceiling height of 2.9 m (9' 6″) used in unit 1 has been continued into the extension, with some improvement in the acoustic panels. The earlier panels have painted surfaces that eliminate most of their acoustic quality and show wear easily. Floor covering is predominantly carpeting, which provides good acoustical control and cuts down on maintenance costs. In areas where carpeting is not feasible, vinyl floor tiles have been used. In the treatment of walls both wood paneling (walnut and birch) and vinyl wall coverings have been used. Areas around recessed drinking fountains have ceramic tiles, as do the cloakrooms. In general, both wall and floor coverings are in keeping with the function of each particular area.

Seating is provided for approximately 1,550 readers. A concentration of informal seating is to be found in the current periodical and lounge areas, while a variety of seating for more serious study is provided in other areas of the library. There are 11 group-study rooms catering to groups of from four to six students. In general they are located near the main staircase on each level. Special attention has been given to acoustic control of these studies, while a glass panel in the door provides visual control. Twenty-three faculty studies are provided at present. These are very popular and twice this number could have been well utilized. They are located primarily on the third level, have individual temperature control, and are ventilated to accommodate smoking without any escape of fumes into adjacent areas. These rooms are assigned to academic staff for periods of up to a year.

Study lounges are located on each level. These are attractively furnished with a variety of seating and provide an excellent study environment (see Fig. 5.8). In addition, a smoking lounge is provided on each level, in proximity to the cloakroom complexes. On the main level there is a pleasant study lounge for faculty. These informal areas are very popular with staff and students, and are well used.

The library has two rooms designated for the use of graduate students. Each has a number of lockers that may be assigned to individuals for storage of library and personal materials. Typing facilities are also provided for the use of students.

Interior design consultants were hired to decorate the interior of the library, and the results are particularly successful. These specialists compiled sample boards of different color and texture combinations for carpeting, fabric, wall coverings, furniture designs, paint colors, and wood finishes. Primary colors were chosen for the furniture—orange, red, purple, blue, green, ochre, and yellow. A rust-colored carpet was selected for the major part of the library, with a brown shaggy carpet in the staff lounge. Curtaining is also a rust color, but of very light sun-filter fabric so as to give a feeling of privacy without blocking visibility. At the time of the expansion, extensive remodeling and redecoration of the existing library took place, so that now the library appears to be continuous in design, appearance, and atmosphere.

ECONOMY

This cubic building is of ideal shape from the point of view of economy. In an academic library where long hours of artificial light and air conditioning are required, this is an important factor, and especially so in Northern Iowa where in summer outside temperatures may be 30° Celsius (86°F) or more. The heating requirement in

Fig. 5.8. University of Northern Iowa Library: Study Lounge

cold weather is not such a great consumer of energy in a deep plan building.[6]

SECURITY

An electronic book detection system has been installed at the main entrance. As regards fire, the library has been fitted with smoke detectors, and should one of these be activated, an alarm will sound initially in the Campus Security Office and thereafter in the City Fire Department. Security staff are able to reach the library within one minute. There are no water sprinklers; fire extinguishers are placed in strategic, easily visible positions on each floor. Emergency stairs and exits are located on each side of the building.

EXTERNAL FEATURES

Externally, both units are finished in Norman-sized brick with concrete block backup. Window frames throughout are aluminum, with insulating glass in window openings to regulate heat gain and loss. Floors are made of reinforced two-way concrete slabs, with reinforced concrete columns spaced to meet the modular system.[7]

ASSESSMENT

The careful planning of this library may be seen in the many small details that make for perfection. Clocks are located throughout the building for the convenience of readers. Coat racks are provided in all study areas and lounges. An intercommunication system, used for public announcements and in cases of emergency, has proved very satisfactory. Generous provision of signs throughout the building makes for ease of use and orientation. Public telephones, both internal and off-campus, are located near the main staircase. There is generous provision of water fountains. Reading areas are designed to give the user a feeling of comfort and they cater to almost every individual preference. A final touch that adds greatly to the atmosphere of the library is the display of many original art works. Iowa State, by law, demands that 0.5% of the building cost of any public building must be spent on art, and in the University of Northern Iowa Library a large, semicircular metal sculpture is suspended between the ceiling of the third level and the floor of the main level. By sculptor Phillip Ogle, and called "Dichotomy," it may not be everyone's taste in art, but it certainly is most impressive. In addition, the University Gallery is unable to display all its holdings, and is happy that the library exhibit paintings, ceramics, and sculpture on a semipermanent basis. It is expected that students and staff alike will benefit from exposure to these works.[8]

In summary, the two most striking architectural achievements of this library are function and ambience. The arrangement of books, readers, and services on each floor is simple and very satisfactory, and major traffic routes are correspondingly logical. The entire building is aesthetically pleasing, comfortable, and inviting to users. A large open access university library demands an orderly arrangement of materials and services if the patron is to operate independently, but this may easily result in a building that is rigid and impersonal. The architects and design consultants of the University of Northern Iowa Library have been unusually innovative in employing materials and design elements that introduce warmth, informality, and beauty. The choice of color and finishes throughout adds up to a pleasing coordination of features and contributes greatly to a positive library experience.

UNIVERSITY OF DENVER LIBRARY

Architects:	Hellmuth, Obata, and Kassabaum (St. Louis, Missouri)
In charge:	Gyo Obata
Interior:	Hellmuth, Obata, and Kassabaum (St. Louis, Missouri)
Gross size:	13,950 m² (150,200 ft²)

Net size:	11,811 m² (127,100 ft²)
Balance area:	2,139 m² (23,100 ft²); 18% of usable space
Book capacity:	2 million items
Seating:	1,400
Total cost:	$4.5 million (fully equipped)
Cost/m²:	$323 (equipped)
Date of completion:	August 1972
Librarian:	M. Schertz

SITE

The University of Denver is situated on the outskirts of the city of Denver, Colorado. Ancient trees, landscaped gardens, and elegant buildings, old and new, combine to create a scholarly and harmonious environment. The library, named the Penrose Library after benefactors of the university, is located at the geographic center of the campus. "From the front steps one sees three generations of libraries in the history of this 110-year-old University in the Carnegie (now the Bookstore); the Mary Reed, one of the most handsome buildings on Campus and now a classroom and faculty office building; and the Penrose, which integrates into the main library previously scattered branch collections."[9] The site provides space for expansion. It is bounded on the west by the student union and on the south by the Humanities Gardens, which give it a particularly fine approach and contribute to its being the focal point of university life.

BRIEF

The librarian (Morris Schertz) and staff of the University of Denver Library prepared an exceptionally good and clearly expressed brief for the architect, Gyo Obata, which gave him the conceptual and philosophical background necessary for the project and assisted him greatly in creating this outstanding library. Their mandate[10] stated that one of the chief purposes of a liberal education is to "make the student feel at home in the realm of learning—to achieve an harmonious integration of his cultural growth with other aspects of his collegiate experience." A library was required that would achieve this goal through being a welcoming, comfortable place that students would naturally enjoy being in, not just for study purposes, but for leisure as well. Requirements of the building as outlined in the brief were:

- that it should have distinction and beauty symbolizing its importance as the center of the University's educational and research activities;
- that it should be economical and efficient in its layout and design, without wasted space and unnecessary monumentality;
- that it should be carefully adapted to the needs of those using it;
- that it avoid ostentation, . . . deriving its excellence from the appropriateness with which it relates to its functions and to its environment;
- that it create an atmosphere which invites student and faculty use.[11]

The planners also noted that modern libraries are no longer merely repositories for books and periodicals but "materials centers" in which all kinds of recorded knowledge is collected and utilized in many different formats. They concluded:

> It is impossible to say what the library of 1995 will be like. Technology has already begun to shake the foundation of university libraries. Whether all these changes will come to fruition is difficult to say. All that we can possibly do today is make certain that the building can absorb change and absorb it in a way which will not demand expensive and costly renovation. The keynote is flexibility.[12]

SIZE AND EXTENDIBILITY

Opened in 1972, the Penrose Library (phase 1) is expected to provide for library needs until 1995, i.e. a period of 23 years. At that stage, expansion will have to take place, and the building has been designed to facilitate the addition of phase 2. The site is also suitable for an expanded building. The planning team detailed the following requirements for the first and second phases of the building program:[13]

	Seats	Books	Staff	m²	ft²
Phase 1:	1,166	1,293,000	146	9,329	100,315
Phase 2:	1,242	1,270,000	6	7,714	82,950
Total (1+2):	2,408	2,563,000	152	17,043	183,265

On completion the building had a gross area of 150,000 ft² and a net area of 127,000 ft². Once phase 2 is completed, it is expected to have a gross area of 275,000 ft² (25,565 m²), and at this stage the building will provide seating for approximately 27% of projected student enrollment.

FLEXIBILITY

In line with this stated requirement, modular design has been utilized, with a bay size of 8.4 m (27′ 6″) through most of the library. With stack ranges placed on 1.22 m (4 ft) centers, seven ranges are possible within each bay. Most of the shelving is standard 200 mm (8 ins), thus allowing stack aisles of 810 mm (2′ 8″). Widely spaced columns at regular intervals and the absence of supporting walls help to create flexible space. The fixed elements of toilets, stairs, mechanical rooms, and lifts are located around the perimeter in eight cores. In addition, the library has a live floor load capacity of 7 kN/m² (150 lbs/ft²) throughout, and ventilation outlets are liberally provided so that areas partitioned off are not without air supply. Thus the library is easily able to adapt to changing requirements.

The University of Denver Library has been built on three levels, with the main floor in the center (see Fig. 5.9). Organization of the main floor is the key to efficient library operation. Because this is the most heavily used part of any library and the point of departure for most library patrons, it should be inviting and attractive. It is in both the organization and appearance of this main level that the Penrose Library excells. The functions assigned to this floor and their special interrelationships are critical and complex and have been dealt with by the architect in an uncluttered and logical manner, enabling users to orient themselves quickly upon entering the building.

The lobby is an attractive, spacious area with the circulation desk immediately opposite the entrance and the information desk to the left. Staircases to the upper and lower levels are immediately apparent. An open catalogue area is located to the left of the circulation desk, containing cabinets interspersed with consultation tables holding computer terminals. The lobby also contains bright, informal modular furniture (see Fig. 5.12), in close proximity to an exhibition area composed of movable wooden stands that can hold pictures, books, and other types of material. They are versatile and economical in their use of space. Special lighting has been installed to enhance this display area. Immediately beyond this is a browsing room, providing a quiet environment for readers and containing some current journals and new books. It is sufficiently removed from the circulation desk for traffic not to disturb the reader, yet it is close enough for visual control by the desk staff. Although casual furniture has been provided in the browsing room, it is not arranged in groups, as conversation is discouraged.

The circulation department in the Penrose Library is provided with the space and facilities this focal point deserves yet so seldom receives. "It is here that the patron usually makes his first contact with the Library and a major function is thus a public service one."[14] The department is divided into a circulation counter, records area, shelving area, and circulation office. The staff work areas are partitioned off from the circulation counter so that noise is contained and backroom work is kept from public view. The counter itself is large and well signposted, and very accessible to all entering or leaving the library. Natural traffic routes to lifts, stairways, and other departments in the library (reference, periodicals, information) pass close by the desk, and visual control by circulation staff over a large part of this main floor is possible. The

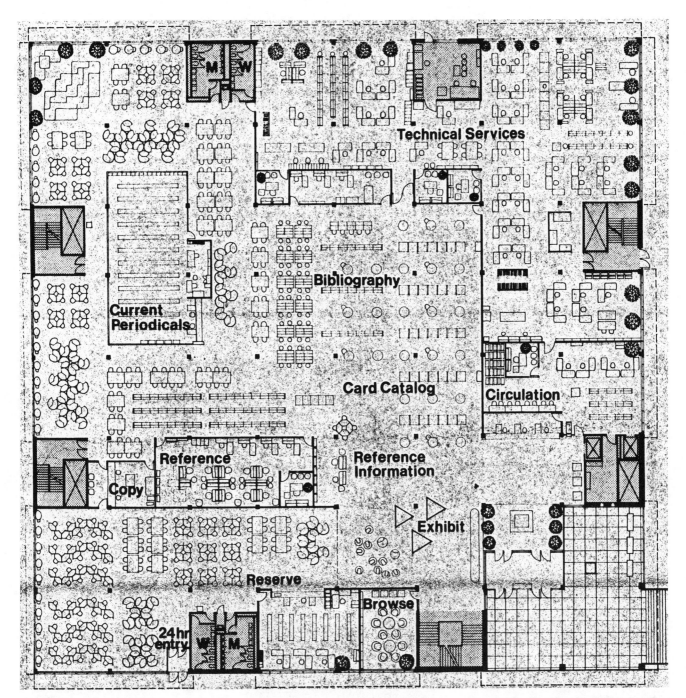

Fig. 5.9. University of Denver Library: Floor Plan, Main Level. By permission from Morris Schertz, Director, Penrose Library, University of Denver.

work area behind adjoins the technical processing area to facilitate the regular communication existing between these two departments. The reshelving area is particularly successful. Here books are sorted in preparation for shelving, and in accordance with the requirements of the brief, 32 single-sided shelving units are provided with a capacity of up to 4,000 volumes. There is space for 25 book trolleys.[15] The area also contains two book return chutes. The book return

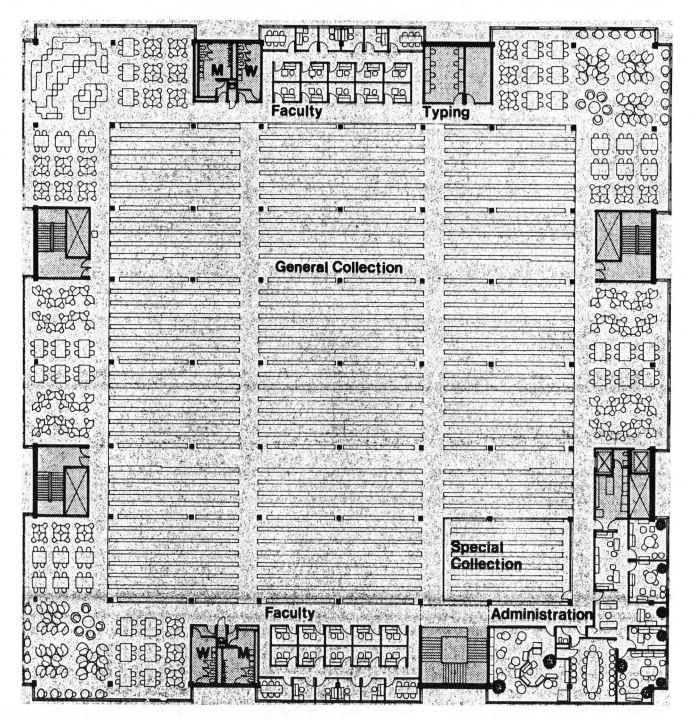

Fig. 5.10. University of Denver Library: Floor Plan, Upper Level. By permission from Morris Schertz, Director, Penrose Library, University of Denver.

slots are situated in the wall close to the public counter and lead directly to the reshelving area, thus facilitating easy traffic flow at the counter.

Between the catalogue area and Technical Processing Department, and in useful proximity to the reference information desk, is the bibliography area. The Current Periodicals Department lies between reference and the serials section of technical processing, and is also in close proximity to the bibliography area. It is well re-

Fig. 5.11. Penrose Library, University of Denver: View of Exterior

Fig. 5.12. Penrose Library, University of Denver: Lobby Area

lated spatially to the bound periodicals collection on the floor below via a nearby staircase and lift.

The reserve collection is also on the main floor. It contains a reading room with its own entrance, and may remain open after hours by means of a sliding screen that separates it from the reserve book collection and the rest of the library.

The Technical Processing Department is ideally located on this main level. The individual departments making up this section (acquisitions, monograph cataloguing, and serials cataloguing) are closely related and linked by the line sequence in which orders for items and the items themselves are handled.[16] Movement from one area to another is unobstructed—serials cataloguing is close to current periodicals; acquisitions and bindery preparation are close to the receiving and shipping room; and the processing area is adjacent to circulation. The interrelationships of this area with others in the library have obviously been carefully considered by the planners and architect, and its location on this busy service level is as close to ideal as one is likely to find.

The lower level consists mainly of stack and study areas. Here are housed the bound periodical, microform, and document collections, as well as part of the book collection. A variety of study stations are located around the perimeter—student and faculty work areas, student conference rooms, individual carrels, typing rooms, smoking areas, and casual seating. An interesting and very practical design feature is that readers may approach the bookstacks directly from the access to the floor (all stairs and lifts) without moving through study or reading areas.[17] The arrangement of stack ranges and aisles is simple and uniform. Major traffic lanes are wide and clearly defined, being logically related to the core areas.

A staffroom and kitchenette are also located on this level, in proximity to a lift and toilets. A variety of furniture is provided, and equipment includes a refrigerator, stove, sink, and vending machine. Good use of color has been made in this room, and it is bright and cheerful.

The third level, like the lower level, contains primarily stack and study areas (see Fig. 5.10).

Also on this level are the administrative suite and Special Collections Department. The former is an attractive area consisting of offices for the director and two assistant directors, a general office and reception area, a conference room for up to 25 people, and a work supply room for stationery and photocopying machines. It is located within easy stair or lift access from the lobby for the convenience of visitors. The special collections/archives area includes both storage space for the material housed here and a small reading room.

INTERNAL ENVIRONMENT

The brief to the architect requested that special care be given to the fenestration in order that the interior be protected from heat gain. Obata's solution to this is particularly interesting. Reflective double-insulated glass has been used that permits one to look out on the campus during the day. At night those outside may see into the library while the users see only the reflected interior. By reflecting the sun's heat, the mirrored windows assist in providing an even climate throughout the year.[18] Window frames are of aluminum.

Particular care was taken regarding illumination in order that the maximum amount of light be provided with a minimum of glare. The lighting consists of "special fluorescent fixtures fitted with deep louvers so that the actual source of light is almost obscured." Thus the impression of the ceiling as the primary source of light is effectively reduced.[19] Intensity of light at the work surface is approximately 75 foot-candles throughout the library. Fixtures are at right angles to stack ranges and placed 1.83 m (6 ft) on centers. In certain areas special requirements have been fulfilled. There is high-intensity lighting at points on the exterior for night use, independent control of ambient lighting in the microform area, and spot lighting in the exhibition area. Electrical lighting circuits on each floor are controlled from a central panel located in the circulation department.[20]

Wiring is contained in conduits placed in a grid 1.83 m (6 ft) on centers. Provision is made for both 110 and 220 volt lines, television, terminals, and other computer equipment.

Air conditioning and ventilation are adequate, maintaining an even temperature and humidity throughout the year. Special air control allows for smoking in certain areas such as staff offices, the browsing room, and student discussion rooms.

A public address system has been installed in the library, with sufficient speakers to enable it to be heard everywhere in the building. It is used only for announcing closing time, fire drills, and for occasional special announcements in emergencies. It is located at the circulation desk, with broadcast equipment locked away when not in use.[21]

Throughout the library, a wide variety of reading, study, and lounge stations have been provided, ranging from individual tables and open rectangular tables, through semiprivate and individual carrels, to group lounge areas.[22] The seating is imaginative, practical, flexible, and comfortable, much of it having been designed by the architect specifically for this library. There are

gaily colored bean bags, semicircular "booths," and "megaform" structures made up of carpet-covered foam cubes arranged in informal descending tiers that create spaces on which students may sit, sprawl, or lie as they wish. There is also the "carola"—a hollow 1.5m (5 ft)-high molded plastic cylinder with a third of the cylinder cut away for the door. A molded plastic desk and seat, upholstered with foam and brightly colored fabric, complete the unit.[23] The majority of student seating consists of individual carolas and carrels. The latter are three-sided, with a work surface approximately 610 mm × 915 mm (2 ft × 3 ft) and a shelf above. Each is provided with a coat hook. There are 28 faculty studies, each 5.6 m² (60 ft²). They are located conveniently close to the stack areas, and each contains a study desk with drawer, side extention for typewriter, chair, shelves, chalkboard, and electrical outlet. They are acoustically controlled, and special attention has been given to ventilation to cater for smoking.

Located on the upper and lower levels are typewriting rooms—16 stations in all—and stu-

Fig. 5.13. Penrose Library, University of Denver: Staff Office

dent conference rooms. The latter are grouped in pairs with a removable center partition to provide a larger space when necessary. Each accommodates up to six students and contains a table, chairs, chalkboard, and coat hooks.

Good use has been made of primary colors in this library and the overall effect is cheerful and inviting. Yellow, orange, and red carpeting provide a striking color key for reading areas on each floor. Carpeting in the large bookstacks is off-white, which helps to lighten these awesome, somewhat densely packed areas. Walls in the reading rooms are painted in colors corresponding to the carpeting, with bright graphic designs that are easily visible and recognizable from the inner stack areas. The interior decorator has created particularly successful staff offices. Many of these are without windows and situated in the internal spaces of the library. They have colorful walls and excellent use has been made of mirrors to create interesting graphics, extend the office visually, and give an impression of space and light (see Fig. 5.13).

Signs have been carefully devised, and the result is very successful. Major service points are indicated in white letters up to 500 mm high. These are highly visible, serve their purpose admirably, and contribute a rather elegant contrast to the bright and informal decor of the main floor. Clear signs containing floor plans and book classification schedules are provided on each level.

ECONOMY

In a similar manner to the University of Northern Iowa Library, the Penrose Library copes fairly well with large variations in outside temperature through having a cubic shape and deep compact design. Heat loss and gain is reduced by the use of double-insulated glass. Economical movement of readers, staff, and books is enhanced through placing the main floor at ground level, with floors above and below. The careful location of various areas in proximity to each other and to the core areas containing stairs and lifts has further reduced unnecessary movement and waste of time.

EXTERNAL FEATURES

The exterior of the building has a simple elegance. To achieve this, materials were limited to three—precast concrete of earth-brown color that harmonizes with existing campus buildings, reflective glass, and aluminum door and window frames.[24] Conspicuously placed alongside the pathway to the main entrance of the library is a large sculpture consisting of two gracefully linked ovals of steel, 4 m in diameter. The sculptor was Charles O. Perry, and the work was donated to the library jointly by the architects and the building contractor.

The building is unusual in that fast-track (phased) construction was used. This is a concept involving a team approach, a merger of architect and builder. It provides for a stipulated time schedule in the planning and construction phases of the building, and these two elements are carried out simultaneously. The control of time is important, enabling more accurate cost predictions for labor and materials, and making it possible to build for a specific agreed-to price. This was important to the University of Denver, which had promised the donor of the gift of $4.5 million a fully furnished building of 13,950 m² (150,000 ft²).[25] A building contractor was appointed in whom the librarian, Schertz, had confidence, and he in turn subcontracted the design of the library to an architect. This paid dividends, "as architect Obata, in bidding for the contract, was forced to produce most of his design and commit considerable time to the project before the contract was signed."[26] It is believed that this is the first time this rapid form of construction has been used for a library, providing the advantages of both speed and economy. Approximately one year after groundbreaking, the move into Penrose Library was completed and it was opened to students and faculty—surely a record in the history of academic library construction. However, Schertz[27] warns:

Although phased construction worked for us and we would use the technique again if there were a need for a new building, it is not a technique one should decide upon lightly. There is insufficient time to debate and consider alternatives. The building program must be very specific in order to avoid confusion. Further, there is no possibility of using a committee. Responsibility for decisions must rest with one individual.

ASSESSMENT

The only question that may be asked about this library concerns the stack areas on the upper and lower floors. These are very large, and the aisle width of 810 mm (2′ 8″) is narrow. The planners realized this but felt that it would be adequate. Others are less convinced.[28] The sheer size of the stacks is intimidating. Wider aisles might have made them less so, although of course some storage space would have been lost. The planners also required that islands of seating within the stacks be avoided so as not to break the logical continuity of the arrangement, yet one suspects that some seating might have improved the general environment and provided a useful facility for those browsing in the stacks.

All other aspects of this library are very positive. It has qualities of flexibility, organization, and comfort that make it exceptional in many ways, and this is demonstrated in the heavy use made of its facilities by staff and students alike. It is also bold, inviting, and colorful, providing spaces of unusual quality that are a delight to the visitor. Most impressive is the way in which the architect observed and catered to the functions of each designated area, relating each carefully and accurately to others associated with it. In this, his work was facilitated by an excellent brief that provided him with very specific detail as well as the necessary philosophical objectives. The result is a truly functional layout that could be used with confidence as a basis of design by library planners. The choice of Obata, an experienced architect with many award-winning designs to his name, has paid off handsomely, and the University of Denver has a library of distinction and beauty that is certain to accept gracefully the changes and developments that will inevitably affect it in the future.

REFERENCES

UNIVERSITY OF NORTHERN IOWA LIBRARY

1. University of Northern Iowa, *"Program of Requirements for an Expanded Library Building at the University of Northern Iowa, Cedar Falls, Iowa."* Revised final draft, by D.O. Rod (Cedar Falls: University Library, 1971), p.7 (unpublished).
2. Ibid., p.21.
3. Personal communication from D.O. Rod, librarian, University of Northern Iowa Library, when I visited this library in September 1984.
4. Ibid.
5. University of Northern Iowa Library, *Fact Sheet.* 1984. (Unpublished).
6. H. Faulkner-Brown, "The open plan and flexibility," *International Association of Technological University Libraries*, Proceedings, vol.11, 1979, p.8.
7. D.O. Rod, *"University of Northern Iowa Library"* (n.d., unpublished), p.14 (outline specification).
8. Personal communication from D.O. Rod.

UNIVERSITY OF DENVER LIBRARY

9. University of Denver Penrose Library [Brochure on the Penrose Library describing the building and its construction.] (n.d.), p.4.
10. University of Denver Libraries, *"Building Program, Phase One."* Denver, Colo., 1971 (unpublished), p.1.
11. Ibid.
12. Ibid., p.2.
13. Ibid., pp.11–16.
14. Ibid., p.21.
15. Ibid.
16. Ibid., p.64.
17. Ibid., p.84.
18. University of Denver Penrose Library, p.4.
19. "Penrose Library," *Interior Design*, April 1973, p.124.
20. University of Denver Libraries, *"Building Program,"* p.6.
21. Ibid., p.9.
22. "Penrose Library," p.124.
23. University of Denver Penrose Library, p.6.
24. "Penrose Library," p.124.
25. M. Schertz, "Two ways of planning: Penrose," *Library Journal*, December 1976, p.2456.
26. "Building portfolio," *College Management*, January 1973, p.30.
27. Schertz, p.2457.
28. Discussion with Ralph Ellsworth on visiting this library in September 1984.

6 *South Africa: Case Studies*

UNIVERSITY OF STELLENBOSCH LIBRARY

Architects:	Interplan (Cape Town)
Engineers:	Breinette Kruger and C.A. du Toit (Cape Town)
Floor area:	16,740 m² (180,000 ft²)
Book capacity:	700,000
Storage capacity:	1,000,000
Reader stations:	1,500
Cost:	R12.5 million
Completion date:	November 1983
Librarian:	F. du Plessis

SITE AND ACCESS

The architects were commissioned by Stellenbosch University to design a new library that would replace the old Carnegie Library and incorporate a number of branch libraries and departmental collections located elsewhere on the campus. Siting the new library was a problem, as there was no available space on the campus, and the town of Stellenbosch has to all intents and purposes reached a stage of zero growth. It is surrounded by agricultural land and is unable to grow much beyond its present limit. Consequently it was initially suggested that the existing library building be demolished and a new building constructed in phases, so that library services could continue to operate. However, the sheer size of the building required by the university was not compatible with the scale of Jan Marais Square, which the Carnegie Library overlooked, nor with the size of the surrounding low-rise buildings.[1] Jan Marais Square nevertheless does form the demographic, logistic, and visual focal point of the campus (see Fig. 6.1). The surrounding buildings, although of differing archi-

tectural form, give it a distinctive harmony and character. Perhaps most importantly, the square is within seven minutes walking distance of all teaching departments on the campus.

It was thus decided that this area had to be the answer to the site problem, and various design options were considered by the architects. The proposal finally submitted to the university was to build the library on two levels underground beneath the square. This would retain all the buildings facing the square, including the Carnegie Building, and it would also retain the central open space. A number of universities have utilized this solution in recent years to preserve an area with historical character in which an above-ground structure would be disruptive, for example Harvard, Yale, the University of Illinois (Urbana), the University of Michigan (Ann Arbor) in the United States, and the University of British Columbia in Canada.[2] Although radical in terms of South African library design, this solution solved the university's problem of site, met the library's need for maximum contiguous space, and also provided ample room for expansion.

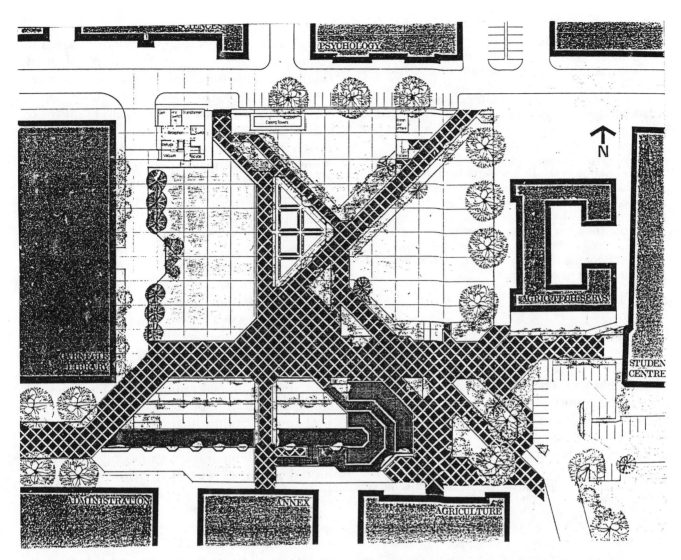

Fig. 6.1. University of Stellenbosch Library: Site Plan. By permission from J.H. Viljoen, Director of Library Services, Stellenbosch University.

THE ARCHITECT'S BRIEF

The brief to the architect described the aims and functions of the university library.[3] It was to form an integral part of the total research and study facilities offered by the university. The previous library system consisted of a central library, four branch libraries, and 19 departmental collections, for the most part administered centrally. It was hoped that in terms of efficient service and costing, the new building would bring about a rationalization of library services and a reduction in the number of departmental libraries. A system of subject librarians would

hopefully encourage this. In the brief, the architects were given details of Faulkner-Brown's "desirable qualities" for a library building—flexibility, compactness, variety, comfort, accessibility, expandibility, organization, security, and function—and were expected to meet these in their proposed plan.

Discussion between the librarian, university planners, and the architects resulted in the following major design objectives:[4]

- to satisfy the stated needs of maximum contiguous space, a high degree of flexibility, and a totally modular plan;

- to design a library in accordance with the latest library design philosophy, i.e. organized on the basis of a number of subject libraries housed in a single building with centralized library services;
- to provide a service infrastructure to cope with present and future needs for audiovisual material, computerization and other technological advances;
- to create an environment conducive to study as well as relaxation with particular care being taken in the creation of a psychologically acceptable subterranean building;
- to create space of such quality as to improve the frequency of use of the library;
- to design an energy-efficient building;
- to design a civic space of quality retaining the integrity of the Square.

ENGINEERING REQUIREMENTS

These are of particular interest in an underground library. The contract engineers[5] conducted a ground investigation of the area in mid-1980 and found that although ground water was present, underground construction was possible if certain preconditions were met:

- external walls should be as impermeable as possible to ensure the greatest degree of waterproofing;
- module size should be optimal, both from a library planning and a cost point of view;
- surfaces should be as inexpensive as possible without affecting mechanical services;
- the construction should be simple;
- the building should be serviceable as regards likely user needs.

Waterproofing. Underground buildings invariably have greater potential for water leakage than their counterparts above the surface. Apart from the inconvenience of leakage, costs associated with water damage repair are high, and it is essential to construct a good waterproofing system.[6] The walls of the library consist of three layers: an outer layer of durable damp-proof material, an outer wall 200 mm (8ins)-thick of waterproof reinforced concrete, separated by a space from the inner wall. This enables any water entering the area to be drained off. Regarding the foundations, an underground

drainage system has been constructed to ensure that there is no pressure on the floor. Above this drainage system is a durable waterproof membrane that adjoins the walls and is covered with a 50–75 mm (2–3 ins) layer of gravel. On top of this is a layer of waterproof concrete on which the columns stand. There is then a layer of loose rough brick, followed by another waterproof membrane, and finally, the concrete floor. The columns themselves are set in "trays" and are carefully protected from damp.

Above the 400 mm (16 ins)-thick waterproof roof is a durable waterproof membrane attached to the walls. This is covered with a 75 mm (3 ins) layer of gravel to protect it. The roof is built with a slight downward slope from the center (1 : 200) to facilitate drainage. All water drained from the outer surfaces of the building is led via gravitational piping to the pumphouse, from which it is pumped into the general storm water system. A reserve pump is provided, which starts automatically should the main pump fail.[7] This complex construction of the outer walls also helps to prevent condensation which can become a problem when the surrounding earth is cooler than the internal air temperature. Air conditioning and humidity control (described below) also assist in this respect.

Air conditioning and ventilation. The underground construction of two large spaces creates certain unusual aspects. The influence of daily and seasonal temperature changes is reduced to a large degree because the large mass of earth surrounding the structure modifies the effect of rapid fluctuations in outdoor temperature.[8] The building reacts very slowly to any change, and sudden changes have no effect whatsoever. The costs of cooling are thus low, and are estimated at a third to half the costs of a similar building above ground. The building is thus efficient in terms of energy consumption, and running costs are low. The air conditioning system dissipates the heat build-up caused by the presence of people and lighting in the large internal areas, making use of cool outside air whenever possible.

Central vacuum system. A central vacuum system has been installed for cleaning purposes which has a number of advantages over the traditional method:[9]

- it is quick, with the result that less cleaning staff are required;
- all dust is transported in pipes to the machine area;
- noise level is low;
- ongoing costs are reasonably low;
- no storage space is necessary for equipment;
- the system has a long life.

Outlet pipes are located on columns on a level above the height of the bookshelves. They will thus not influence any future change in the location of the stacks, and flexibility will not be affected.

Elevator installation. There are two elevators in the library. One is for passengers and book trolleys traveling between the two floors, and is located centrally. The other is for goods, used for transporting equipment and parcels from the surface to the two lower levels. Because engine rooms above the elevator shafts at ground level were not desirable from an aesthetic point of view, hydraulic elevators have been installed. The engine rooms are located alongside the elevators and are fitted with soundproofing to lessen noise.

Power network. The electrical power supply to the library is contained within the existing cable network of the campus.[10] Emergency power also had to be supplied for lighting and ventilation, so that activity in the library could continue during a power cut. Special care was taken with the lighting system to facilitate the flexibility required in the open spaces. The continuous single-tube 1.5 m² (16 ft²) light armatures are suspended from the ceiling, the pattern consisting of a square within a square, repeated throughout the reading/stack areas (see Fig. 6.5). Shelving may thus be placed at any angle without reduction in level of illumination.

A bell system has been installed to announce closing time, and clocks are placed at suitable intervals.

FLEXIBILITY

The brief stated that the internal planning of the building should make provision for growth and possible rearrangement of areas to provide for future needs.[11] Modular planning was recommended. In response to these requirements, the architects investigated various module sizes. In terms of cost there was found to be very little difference between them, and it was thus decided that the module size thought best from the point of view of library planning should be used. Bays are 7.5 m (24' 6") square and column size is 450 mm (18 ins) square. The result is a high degree of flexibility, with large open spaces. Necessary fixed-function areas include:

- the large plant and mechanical equipment area along the northern side of level one;
- a large area of compact shelving occupying eight modules (450 m²/4,844 ft²) directly beneath this on level two;
- cloakroom facilities on both levels along the east side;
- the atrium, central ramp, and core areas containing elevators and stairways.

The entrance is on the upper level on the south side of the building. On entering the library, the large issue desk, which includes the reserve collection, is to the left in proximity to other staff areas which are located on the west side of the building. An open exhibition area is to the right of the entrance, and beyond this are the subject collections for law, science, and technology (see Fig. 6.2). The law section is separated from science by strategic placing of shelving, and has its own seminar room for the use of staff and students. Two further seminar rooms serve science and technology, and in addition there is a smoking room. The stack arrangement on this level consists primarily of books on the south side, reference works in the middle, and periodicals in the north adjacent to the law collection. Reader stations are situated around and between the stacks. Located in the southeast corner on the upper level are the special collections, which include Africana, rare books, manuscripts, and government publications. There is a built-in safe for very valuable material.

A series of ramps, centrally situated, lead down to level two, most of which is taken up by bookstack and study areas relating to the arts

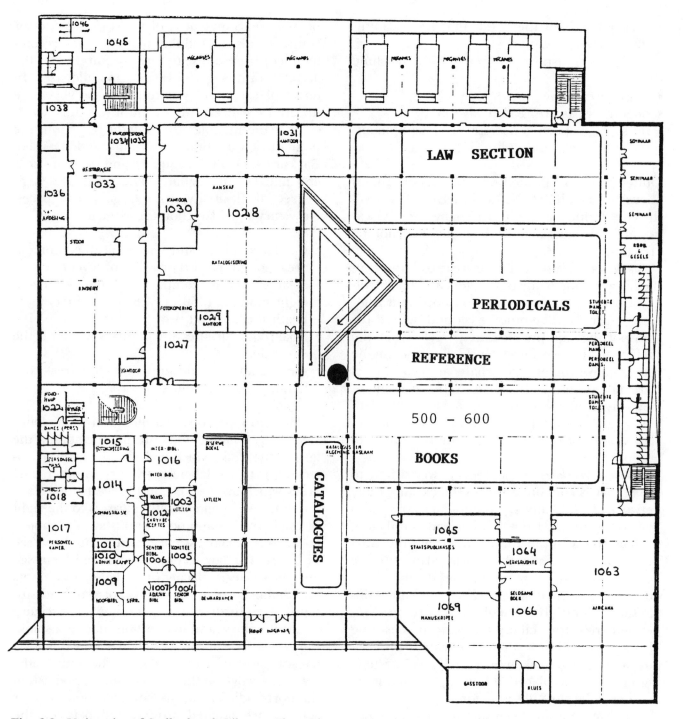

Fig. 6.2. University of Stellenbosch Library: Floor Plan, Level 1. By permission from J.H. Viljoen, Director of Library Services, Stellenbosch University.

and social sciences (see Fig. 6.3). As on the upper level, seminar rooms and cloakrooms are found on the east side, staff areas on the west side, and in the southeast corner, below the protected collections, is a very useful auditorium that seats approximately 146 persons. It is fully equipped audiovisually, with a projection room and remote control console. It is used for library orientation programs, in-service training, meetings, and occasional lectures. Compact shelving is located on the northern side of this lower level.

Although the library is open plan and very

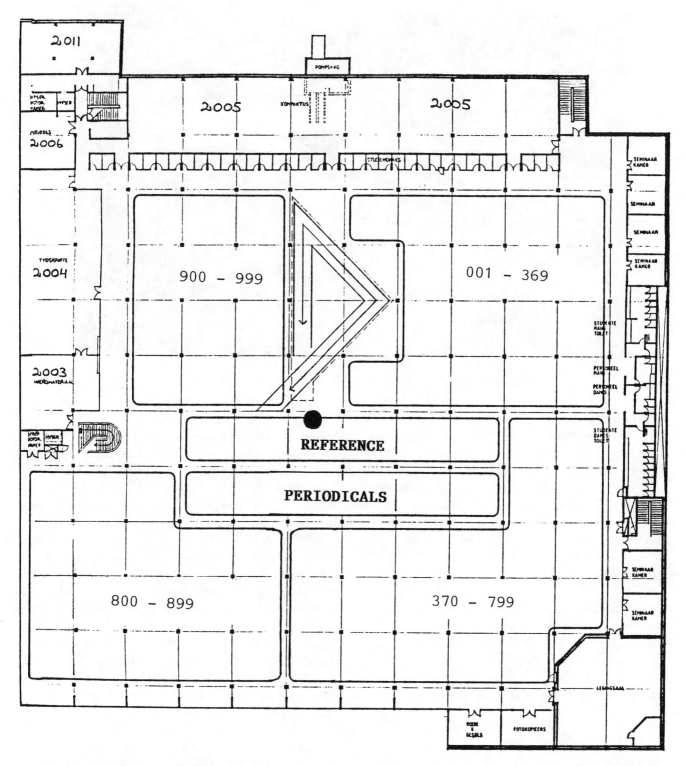

Fig. 6.3. University of Stellenbosch Library: Floor Plan, Level 2. By permission from J. H. Viljoen, Director of Library Services, Stellenbosch University.

Fig. 6.4. University of Stellenbosch Library: View of Exterior

flexible with all office divisions of demountable dry-wall partitioning, flexibility is slightly reduced by areas such as the auditorium with its sloping floor, the large safe and additional fire protection provided in the special collections area, and certain library staff facilities on the west side, e.g. kitchen, cloakrooms with showers, and goods elevator. On the whole, however, the library meets the need for flexibility in the following ways:

- air conditioning and environmental control are adequate throughout;
- the lighting is excellent, and natural lighting is utilized wherever possible;
- the module size lends itself to easy arrangement of book and reader areas.

ORGANIZATION

A library should be organized to allow maximum exposure of readers to information. Ideally reader stations should be interspersed with open access shelving, creating small study areas with a pleasant atmosphere. In the Stellenbosch University Library, an attempt has been made to achieve this kind of atmosphere. The library is well planned, with logical groupings of related services and functions. The major traffic routes are the ramps on the perimeter of the atrium and the stairs on the west, leading to the lower level. There are in addition emergency stairs and exits on the east and north sides, and an exit in the northwest corner for staff only. The main entrance area contains many public services such as interlibrary loans, the photocopying center, general reference collection, a display area, the catalogues, and an information desk. Staff areas occupy the west side of both levels, with departments such as the bindery, restoration center, and acquisitions on level one close to the delivery area and goods elevator. The stacks are arranged so that users may find books, periodicals, and reference works on a particular subject in proximity to each other, with five subject librarians available to provide assistance and information (see Fig. 6.5). On both levels there is a large sign showing the layout of the two floors,

Fig. 6.5. University of Stellenbosch Library: Subject Librarian's Work Station

with subject areas color-coded. The colors coincide with brightly colored discs on the ends of the stacks and suspended from the ceiling, and thus it is easy to locate a subject visually. This aspect of organization has been very successfully achieved in this library.

COMFORT AND VARIETY

Ideally, a library should provide conditions of comfort so that people enjoy using it and work effectively within it. Stellenbosch University Library has provided a variety of seating, including carrels, single tables, group tables, and casual seating. A row of 32 study carrels for postgraduate use separates the compact shelving from the rest of the library on level two. Each contains a desk, chair, shelf, and power point, and is air conditioned and lockable. There are seminar rooms for various types of group use, and smoking rooms are provided for relaxation. On the lower level study spaces look out onto an attractive arrangement of hanging flower boxes on the south and southeast sides, where the ground has

been cut back, and the availability of natural light increases comfort. Natural light also enters through skylights above the atrium, and because these are at the approximate center of the building, they are most effective in improving the internal environment. At no point does one feel that one is in an entirely underground library. The position and structure of the central circulation ramp enable library users to orient themselves easily and provide a point of reference in these somewhat large open spaces. The area around the ramp (and under the skylights) has been attractively decorated with indoor plants and informal furniture. Ramps, a public elevator, and special cloakroom facilities have been provided for handicapped persons.

Approximately 1,500 reader stations are provided in this library. The furniture was custom made, is an attractive combination of chrome and wood, and is entirely flexible in that tables may be joined together to form group study areas, side panels may be added or removed depending on the degree of privacy required, and tables may be grouped in any configuration (see Fig. 6.6). It was interesting to observe while visit-

Fig. 6.6. University of Stellenbosch Library: Flexible Study Carrels

ing this library that the majority of students appeared to prefer the open group study areas to the private carrel desks. Students using the library have a wide choice of study environment and whatever their choice are assured of comfortable, high-quality, and attractive work stations.

SECURITY

Security has been provided in the following ways:

- There is an electronic book detection unit at the main entrance/exit.
- There is only one main entrance/exit to the library for the public, although four exits may be used in an emergency.
- Precautions against fire have been taken. In the special collections area, carbon dioxide gas is provided due to the value of these items, while in the remainder of the library there are

water sprinklers. The building is divided into blocks, and an alarm from a smoke detector activates only one block. The alarm system is linked by computer to Campus Security, and a seven-minute delay period between the initial alarm and the activation of the sprinkler enables a security guard to investigate the area and turn off the system unless its activation is absolutely necessary. Although not ideal, it was required that water sprinklers be installed in accordance with the regulations of the local fire department.

EXTERNAL FEATURES

As may be seen from both the site plan (Fig. 6.1) and the view of the exterior (Fig. 6.4), the library is visible on the south side, where the ground has been cut back to allow natural light to enter the building. Lack of natural light is one of the most frequent criticisms of underground libraries. The difficulty of orientation in windowless areas can result in a number of negative psychological reactions, which may include fear of structural collapse, fear of being trapped underground, or claustrophobia.[12] At Stellenbosch, many of these negative effects have been compensated for through excellent design. The internal environment has been greatly improved by creating pleasant views from windows on the south and east sides. Attractive landscaping, brick paving, retaining walls, and the planting of vegetation have all had a positive effect on the users' perception of the library as they approach it. The entrance to the building has been attractively designed, with impressive stairways of semioctagonal shape leading from the square down to the first level. It defines the size and function of the building, serves as a major source of natural light, and links the library to other buildings close by. It is on the major pedestrian and cycle route across the square, with easy access to the student union.

In the north a small section of the library rises above ground level, housing the transformer, the central vacuum system, refuse removal area, and staff entrance. It has been discreetly executed, and does not impose on the open space. The Jan Marais Square, previously neglected and somewhat insignificant, is now the heart of the campus.

EXTENDIBILITY

It was required that the building provide for future expansion. This is physically possible in the new library, but costly. All expansion would be underground, first in a southerly direction toward the administration building, and then eastward toward the student union. However, it is envisaged that the large area of compact shelving on level two, which can accommodate 1 million items, will supply space for lesser-used material for many years. It is also assumed that before any expansion becomes necessary, a cooperative central store will have been established by major libraries in the Western Cape area of South Africa. This would enable the university library to operate on the zero-growth principle.

SPACE STANDARDS

At the time of planning (1979), government SAPSE space norms were not enforced.[13] In line with overseas standards, an area of 2.7 m^2 (29 ft^2) per study station was used for reading areas, and the space required for the bookstacks was based on the total holdings of the library plus projected growth. Departmental and branch libraries were taken into account so that they could be easily accommodated when it became possible to centralize them.

ASSESSMENT

The new library at the University of Stellenbosch, one of the largest underground libraries in the world, is successful for a number of reasons. The architects, concerned with the surroundings as well as with the building, have managed to design a modern and highly functional library in a historic environment without its dominating or detracting from the latter. Landscaping of the square has maintained the basic topography as well as the existing diagonal student traffic pattern, and a sense of continuity has been achieved with the retention of the original statue and sun dial.[14] The entrance has been well conceived, resulting in an area that is attractive, elegant, and welcoming.

The library is thoroughly modern in its organization, structure, and services. Traffic flow is well planned, with natural light emphasizing the central circulation ramp. The placing of certain facilities in the same location on both levels allows for easy orientation. Fully air conditioned, with special attention having been given to acoustic treatment of study areas, the library provides excellent conditions of comfort and a feeling of spaciousness. It is a technologically advanced and energy-efficient building.

Cooperation between the librarian and architect was excellent and regular meetings took place throughout the planning stages of the building. This enabled the solving of problems in the planning stages and had much to do with the very successful library building that exists today.

The University of the Orange Free State Library

Architects: Van der Walt and Fourie (Bloemfontein)
Floor area: 14,000 m² (150,700 ft²)
Book capacity: 660,000
Reader stations: 1,100
Costs: Building: R10 million; Furniture & equipment: R1.25 million
Library opened: July 1983
Librarian: F.J. Potgieter succeeded by H. de Bruin during the period of planning and construction.

SITE AND ACCESSIBILITY

The University of the Orange Free State (Bloemfontein) has one of the most modern library buildings in Southern Africa, situated on the western edge of the university campus (see Fig. 6.7). During the early stages of planning (1976), student enrollment was increasing rapidly and projections indicated that it would in all likelihood reach a level of 10,000 by the year 1990. Extensions to the existing campus were planned accordingly, and it was supposed that the new library would eventually be centrally placed in a greatly enlarged campus. However, for sociopolitical reasons the university is not expanding at the predicted rate and the student population has decreased in recent years. Numbers are expected to level off at approximately 7,000, and a zero-growth situation is envisaged. Thus, unfortunately, it is likely that the library will remain on the edge of this widespread campus, isolated from a number of academic departments, and remote from the student residences which are for the most part on the eastern side.

The library and the education building alongside it are separated from the remainder of the campus by a road running north-south, which is at a lower level than the campus. The two linking bridges, one on either side of the library, are at campus level. These access roads accommodate both vehicular and pedestrian traffic, and are continuations of the original major thorough-

fares of the university campus. Thus poor accessibility is limited by distance rather than access routes.

SIZE AND EXTENDIBILITY

In relation to its student population, the University of the Orange Free State campus occupies a large area, with an abundance of land available for expansion. Consequently few buildings contain more than three or four levels, and the clearly defined lines of the multilevel library stand out prominently against the skyline (see Fig. 6.8). Although controversial in some aspects of its design, it has a somewhat imposing exterior with smooth, uncluttered lines, recessed windows, and a deep rectangular shape. It is divided in the center by an oval central service core and system of linking walkways. External walls are of pale grit-blasted concrete.

At the time of planning, SAPSE space norms[15] had not yet been introduced and the required capacity of the library was calculated according to those standards outlined by Metcalf. The proposed size of the library was, however, reduced due to financial restrictions. The reduction in size had the effect of bringing it more into line with the SAPSE space norms operative today, and also resulted in a more realistically sized library in view of the zero-growth situation in student numbers. There is accommodation for 660,000 items and study space for 1,100 readers, approximately 16% of the student population. There are three branch libraries—medicine, agriculture, and music—that provide space for subject collections and reader accommodation in addition to that provided by the central library.

FLEXIBILITY

The library is modular, with a bay size of 9 m (29′ 6″). Although open plan in its construction, flexibility of the building is reduced by its division into two separate sections. The communications tower is in the center—a wide core containing an impressive series of ramps as well as public elevators, toilets, and foyer areas (see Fig.

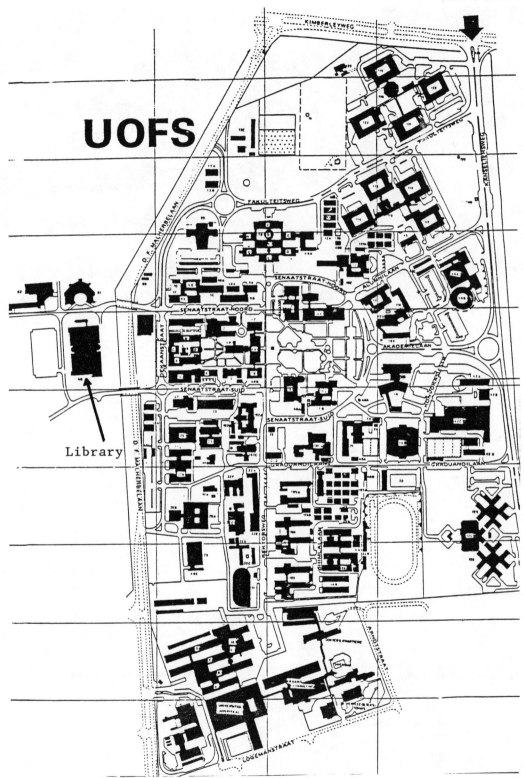

Fig. 6.7. University of the Orange Free State Library: Site Plan. *Source:* "Die Biblioteek." Bloemfontein (South Africa): University of the Orange Free State. By permission from A.J. Viljoen, Directory of Library Services, University of the Orange Free State.

Fig. 6.8. University of the Orange Free State Library: View of Exterior. *Source:* "Die Biblioteek." Bloemfontein (South Africa): University of the Orange Free State. By permission from A.J. Viljoen, Directory of Library Services, University of the Orange Free State.

6.9). The northern block contains administrative and processing offices, staff accommodation of various kinds, the audiovisual department, and special collections. The southern block contains the circulation area, the majority of bookstacks, readers' services departments, and study areas. The structure of the building effectively limits

expansion of an area in one section into space in the other. In addition, the floors on either side of the central core are at differing levels, so that one is required to use the ramps or elevators when moving from one side to the other. Flexible use of space is thus affected and traffic in the central area is increased. It is not clear what the

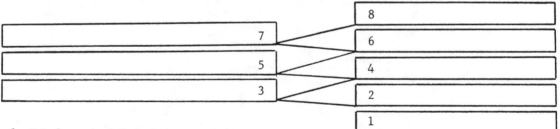

1. Bindery and Receiving
2. General Administration, Acquisitions
3. Lending, General Reference, Photocopying
4. Cataloguing, Management
5. Stack/Reading Room
6. Africana and Protected Collections, Audiovisual
7. Stack/Reading Room
8. Lesser-Used Material

Fig. 6.9. University of the Orange Free State Library: North/South Elevation. *Source:* "Die Biblioteek." Bloemfontein (South Africa): University of the Orange Free State. By permission from A.J. Viljoen, Directory of Library Services, University of the Orange Free State.

architect was hoping to achieve by staggering the levels. From an aesthetic point of view it adds interest and character to the building, but in practical terms no purpose is served.

The circulation area (level three) and the major reading and stack rooms (levels five and seven) are however very flexible within themselves (see Fig. 6.12). They consist for the most part of large open spaces, functionally divided to accommodate different activities and services. Ducting for wiring and cabling is located in the ceiling, and power for the use of electrical or computer equipment is available at any point, being carried in "power columns" or poles that extend from the ceiling to desk surface or floor level. These are flexible and very practical. The power supply is not linked directly to the general electricity supply system, so it is unaffected by fluctuations and is consequently very regular and ideal for computer purposes. All partitioning is demountable and may be removed or easily altered should this be necessary.

FLOOR LAYOUT

Level one, the lowest level of the northern block, contains the delivery area, accessible to vehicular traffic, at the back of the building; a fumigation room for the treatment of donations; an area of compact shelving for the storage of items awaiting processing; a rubbish removal room; and bindery. The latter is on the east side, and good natural light enters through windows on the north and east walls. Also at this level is the machinery for the automatic vacuum system, and occupying a large area to the south, the plant for the air conditioning system. There is also an emergency generator on this level. This floor is compact and well designed, isolating to a large degree from the rest of the building those functions requiring heavy and/or noisy machinery.

Level two is at ground level. An impressive main entrance to the library overlooks an attractive paved patio area with fountains, and pathways and ramps lead from both access roads and the car park. The entrance foyer is a large tiled area with access to the auditorium, overnight reading room, and exhibition hall. The auditorium seats 76 people and is well equipped audiovisually. It is envisaged that in addition to library use, it will be used by academic staff and the public. Swivel chairs are provided so that smaller groups may make use of the area, and there is acoustic damping on the walls to reduce noise level. The exhibition hall/art gallery on the west is also a public area, and it is hoped that these facilities will assist in developing the library as a cultural center on the campus and in the city.[16] Also on level two are general administration offices, a storeroom, and the book and periodical acquisition departments. The staff elevator from level one is in close proximity to the latter departments for easy delivery of parcels.

Level three is the main service level of the library, approached via a ramp from the entrance foyer (see Fig. 6.10). A very large issue desk projects into the center of the area; it is so large that one wonders whether it could in fact decrease efficiency. Opposite the desk is the catalogue and information section and a large reading room fitted with movable screens that provide more intimate study spaces. The general reference collection is housed on the west side. Also on this level are two seminar rooms, a storeroom, photocopying center, and reserve book collection and reading room. There are display areas on both sides of the main hall, as well as an informal reading room where popular magazines are housed. This public service area is well planned. Cognizance has been taken of possible noise disturbance (for example the photocopying machines have been placed in a separate room), and busy informal areas have been placed in close proximity to each other.

Level four, like level two below, is primarily a staff area. The cataloguing department is located on the west side, a staff common room and kitchen in the center, and around the perimeter are the administrative offices. These include a reception area, the librarian's office, his research office, two deputy librarians' offices, a committee room, computer room, the public relations department, and personnel.

On level five are three information service points staffed by subject librarians located close to the catalogues and reference collections. The law collection on the east side, although housed

Fig. 6.10. University of the Orange Free State Library: Entrance to Level 3. By permission from A.J. Viljoen, Directory of Library Services, University of the Orange Free State.

separately, is not physically divided from the rest of the stack/reading room. Level five has been expanded across the central core to level four and an additional study area has been located here. This is not too successful due to the change in floor level. Level seven follows the same general pattern as level five. Periodicals are located toward the center, books are housed in the outer stack areas, and reader stations are around the perimeter where natural light enters the building through large windows. On both levels there are two seminar rooms, a photocopying room, smoking room, lockable study carrels, and a number of casual chairs.

Level six contains a large audiovisual section with 86 carrels, a storage area, and service counter. All carrels have been fitted to accommodate audiocassette players, 65 will accommodate tape/slide equipment if necessary, and 25 are fitted with monitors for video playback. There are also five microform readers. A total of R209,000 was spent on audiovisual equipment (1983), and the UOFS Library has taken a keen interest in pro-

moting the use of this kind of material. I feel, however, that the carrels are a little too small for students to work in comfortably, and more space per unit should have been provided. All software is housed on closed access, and is issued to users at the service counter. The other half of this level is occupied by the special collections department, with a large closed access Africana stackroom, a service counter, reading room, the banned books and theses collections on closed access, and a photocopying facility.

Level eight above houses lesser-used material. There are photocopying facilities, a service counter, and eleven lockable study carrels. In the northeast corner is a large area of compact shelving.

INTERNAL ENVIRONMENT

Air conditioning is provided throughout the building, with a small stand-by unit in case of failure of the main system. A wide variety of seating and study stations has been provided for users. In addition to audiovisual carrels, there are carrel desks in the reading areas, lockable study carrels for use by academic staff and postgraduate students, five seminar rooms for the convenience of lecturers utilizing library materials in their teaching, some relaxation areas, as well as easy chairs distributed throughout the library. The overnight reading room on the ground floor makes provision for students to study without disturbance, and is open 24 hours a day.

Floors are for the most part carpeted in bright green tiles, which bring color and warmth to the internal spaces. The core areas, foyers, and major traffic routes are finished in ceramic tiles, as is the area surrounding the issue desk. In the case of the latter where there is heavy traffic, the ceramic tiles will wear better than carpeting, but loaded book trolleys passing over this area will certainly increase the noise level in this section of the library.

An interesting feature regarding furniture is the method used to distinguish between two types of service counter in the library. All document delivery counters, e.g. issue desks and interlibrary loans, have melamine surfaces, while information counters, e.g. subject librarians and inquiry desks, are comprised of modular wooden units.[17]

SECURITY

Book theft is discouraged by the use of a double-gate electronic book detection system at the main exit point on level three. There are fire escapes on three sides of the building, which are architectural features in that they repeat, on a very much smaller scale, the oval shape of the central communications tower. They may also be used by students for convenient internal access to other levels of the library. The fire protection system consists of sprinklers in the basement (level one) only, and smoke detectors linked to a central control panel on all other levels. From the control panel, which is located behind the issue desk, signals are relayed to the university's security department.

Fig. 6.11. University of the Orange Free State Library: System of Linking Ramps. By permission from A.J. Viljoen, Directory of Library Services, University of the Orange Free State.

ASSESSMENT

The new library building at the University of the Orange Free State is impressive. Although it tends to dominate other buildings on the campus, it does so in a dignified way, and certainly in time this feeling will diminish with the "softening" of some of its sharp angles. Landscaping and the growth of trees and gardens in the vicinity are already helping in this respect. The library's internal spaces are generally well utilized, with functional juxtaposition of various departments and services. It can be clearly seen that much thought and care went into the planning, and for the most part it is successful. Noteworthy aspects of this library, both positive and negative, are mentioned below:

• The site of the library is far from ideal; it was chosen in terms of a future that may never materialize.

• The structural division down the center of the building reduces flexibility and this could impose limitations on the librarian in the future when changes become necessary.

• Although it may be convenient in many respects to separate staff and administrative areas from the public reading and stack areas, the splitting of the building in this way limits effective expansion of user areas. Despite the use of subject librarians on each public level, many professional staff are isolated from library users, in particular their academic colleagues. Informal communication should be encouraged, and this is easier in an environment where there is more possibility for contact.

• The large, open entrance area with deep wells extending from levels two to seven could prove noisy, and is also wasteful of space.

• Traffic routes are simple, and are the same on each floor, thus avoiding confusion on the part

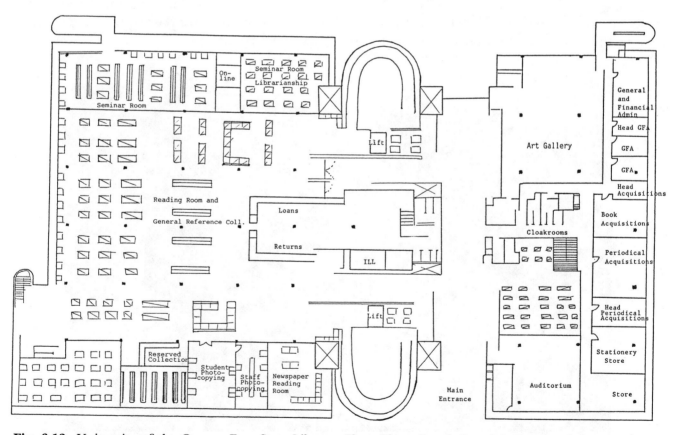

Fig. 6.12. University of the Orange Free State Library: Floor Plans, Levels 2 and 3. By permission from A.J. Viljoen, Directory of Library Services, University of the Orange Free State.

of the user. The main routes are the ramps on the east and west sides of the building (see Fig. 6.11). These are suspended from the roof, are aesthetically very attractive, and also very impressive, but they utilize a lot of space, and distances covered are great. Do the students really make use of them beyond level three, or do they overcrowd the few public elevators provided? On the other hand, a visually open route maintains user orientation while moving between floors, and can perform an important psychological function.

- A good feature is the staff elevator, located in the central core of the northern block, which connects all levels with the delivery area and service entrance on level one.
- The location of compact shelving and lesser-used material on the top floor is practical, and preserves more accessible space for active collections.
- The arrangement of staff areas is thoughtfully and functionally conceived.
- Finally, in view of the growth of academic library collections in this country, the library could perhaps have benefited in the long term from more generous provision of storage space. Now that there are space restrictions imposed on academic libraries, one tends to look on large foyers, deep stair wells, and wide, spacious ramps as being somewhat wasteful of space that could possibly be better utilized. But this tendency is regrettable because it is often such features that give a university library building the symbolic importance it deserves in its academic environment.

REFERENCES

UNIVERSITY OF STELLENBOSCH LIBRARY

1. Interplan, "*University of Stellenbosch: New Library*" (Cape Town: Interplan, n.d.).
2. R. Fuhlrott, "Underground libraries," *College and Research Libraries*, May 1986, p.238.
3. Universiteit van Stellenbosch, "Universiteits-biblioteek: *Program en Akkomodasieskedule vir die Nuwe Biblioteekgebou*," by P. Aucamp (Stellenbosch: Universiteitsbiblioteek, 1979), pp.1–5 [unpublished].
4. Interplan.
5. Universiteit van Stellenbosch, "*Nuwe Biblioteekgebou: Samevatting van Ingenieursverslag*" (Stellenbosch: Stellenbosch University, n.d.) [unpublished].
6. Fuhlrott, p.239.
7. Personal communication with Dr. H. Viljoen (deputy librarian at the time) on a visit to this library during the construction period, 1983.
8. Fuhlrott, p.239.
9. Universiteit van Stellenbosch, "*Nuwe Biblioteekgebou.*"
10. Ibid.
11. Universiteit van Stellenbosch, "Universiteits-biblioteek," p.4.
12. Fuhlrott, p.240.
13. The South African Secondary Education Information system was introduced at universities in 1979. SAPSE space norms for university libraries became operative in the early 1980s.
14. Interplan.

UNIVERSITY OF THE ORANGE FREE STATE LIBRARY

15. The South African Secondary Education Information System. See note 13 above.
16. Personal communication with Dr. H. de Bruin (then librarian) upon visiting this library during the construction period, 1983.
17. Ibid.

7 Centralized or Decentralized Library Planning?

A problem that has confronted librarians often both in the past and still today is the question of how much centralization/decentralization will best suit a particular library and university. The merits and disadvantages of both systems have been argued many times by librarians, and their conclusions, as may be expected, differ widely (e.g. Bryant at Harvard for decentralization, and Smith at Boston against). A review of these arguments and conclusions may assist librarians in considering their own situations, and will hopefully provide some assistance in resolving them.

Librarians are frequently caught between conflicting pressures. On the one hand university administrators desire to hold duplication of collections and dispersal of services to a minimum, while on the other faculty members press for local departmental libraries. In planning new construction and considering changes in existing space utilization, librarians must decide whether it is more efficient to centralize or to decentralize operations. Combining libraries into a central facility may cost less, yet there is a cost in time, energy, and decreased use resulting from locating services too far away from users.[1] It becomes obvious when reading the literature on this subject that each university librarian must take cognizance of local conditions before implementing or changing policy. Metcalf[2] states:

> As long as there are universities with large libraries, the question of centralization or decentralization will be a live topic for discussion, and . . . the question will never be settled permanently one way or the other.

Decentralization may take place on two bases:

- kinds or forms of materials, such as rare books, maps, and audiovisual material;
- user- and subject-oriented materials, such as laboratory collections, subject divisional libraries, and professional school libraries.

The first kind of decentralization is not as contentious an issue as the second. Materials contained in rare book or audiovisual collections are frequently housed separately but within a central library, and they are unlikely to arouse the strength of feeling in faculty staff that a subject collection will. It is user- and subject-oriented decentralization that becomes a major planning criterion in most established university libraries.

Wells[3] recognizes five main types of decentralized collection: branch, subject, departmental, class or seminar, and institute. These develop for various reasons in universities throughout the world. The question of their continued existence arises periodically when changing circumstances on university campuses call for a reassessment of library services. Tauber[4] suggests that the following conditions give rise to a reexamination of the subject:

- constantly rising costs of academic library operation;
- development of new libraries;
- absorption of academic units and their libraries in expanding university departments;
- development of entirely new campuses.

Two further conditions could be:

- the accelerated growth of library collections, leading to critical space shortages;
- the type of library service planned for the future and the proposed use of computer-based technology.

A university librarian faced with changing circumstances of this nature must give consideration to the various arguments for and against centralization, remembering that they are purely theoretical until measured against a particular set of circumstances. The basic criterion should always be library service. How can the library provide the best service in the most economical and effective way? Both viewpoints will be discussed, as both are valid and deserve the attention of the library planner.

Arguments for Centralization

1. **Cost.** In a centralized library funds are not wasted through excessive duplication of materials and a profusion of service points that must be staffed for increasingly long hours of opening. To illustrate the latter, Wagman[5] has stated: "Fully 30% of the personnel budget of my library system is spent in staffing the many branches in less than adequate fashion." It is generally assumed, although not proved, that a centralized system is also more economic in terms of space and equipment.

2. **Staff.** As small a unit as the departmental library is too often staffed by a nonprofessional assistant who is not qualified by either training or experience to interpret the collection to the library's public. In addition to this problem of staff quality, staff quantity also causes difficulties. The one-person library is commonplace. If that person is a professional, he/she cannot be employed economically because a large portion of time must be spent in clerical routines. Professional or not, a single library employee is undesirable from an administrative standpoint because of the difficulty of providing relief staff in the event of absence. Furthermore, the library suffers from discontinuity of policy and practice that is inevitable when staff change, as they frequently do under these circumstances.[6]

3. **Efficiency.** A central library permits supervision of all library activities by trained personnel and assistance and service may be standardized and maintained at a high level. Rather than moving from one library to another, users will find all the material they require in one place; consequently less time is wasted by staff and students and in transferring books from library to library. Efficiency may be further improved by generous provision for loans and a prompt messenger service.

4. **Accessibility.** A central library makes available and equally accessible to all departments the various book collections of the institution. No department should have the right to exclusive possession of any book if it is potentially useful to readers in other departments.

5. **Interdisciplinary approach.** There is a growing interdependence of knowledge, and this is reflected in research and education. This approach may be encouraged and facilitated in a central library, while fractionalization of the collection into branch libraries has the opposite effect. Bruno[7] points out: "With the concept of the unity of knowledge, especially in the sciences, departmental libraries are giving way to a larger subject division approach."

6. **Communication.** Communication on the university campus is hindered by a branch library system. A central library, on the other hand, provides a meeting place for faculty and staff of all departments, making for a feeling of fellowship in scholarly pursuits and encouraging cross-fertilization of ideas.

7. **Convenience.** Although the idea of bringing library materials on a particular subject closer to those studying it is attractive, there is in reality no one place where all material on a subject may be found. A certain journal

may be of use to students in a variety of disciplines, and a single assignment could take the enterprising student all over the campus in his search for material. Watts[8] states: "Sound, scholarly research is hard, detailed and exhausting work. But let's not make it any harder by carving up knowledge and separating it unnecessarily by placing it all over campus."

8. **Attitudes and educational significance.** Staff and students using a departmental library tend to regard it as theirs, and do not see it as a subject section of the larger university collection. As a consequence they may either remain ignorant or fail to exploit the resources of the library system as a whole.[9] As regards library staff attitudes, branch libraries can create unhealthy loyalties to the welfare of a given branch and the department or faculty with which it is associated rather than to the library and its collection as a whole.

9. **Technology.** Improved and more sophisticated machine-based services may be offered in a central library. Because of the cost of equipment and expertise on the part of personnel (e.g. online information service), it is frequently impossible to extend these to branches.

10. **Administrative control.** Coordination, cooperation, and communication are difficult to achieve in a widely dispersed library system.

11. **Adequacy.** It is inevitable that departmental book funds will be inadequate to supply all that is wanted in a departmental library no matter how wisely money is managed. No departmental library can be fully self-sufficient.

12. **Response to change.** It is often impractical to pattern library structure on the administrative organization of the university. The distribution of courses among departments sometimes changes; academic staff may move between departments taking their subject specialities with them; departments may move from one building to another; new departments are established and others may be discontinued. Central libraries and their services are unaffected by these changes.

ARGUMENTS FOR DECENTRALIZATION

Is one central place on the campus where all library and information materials are housed necessarily the best configuration?

1. **Cost.** The costs of decentralization are more talked about than studied.[10] The apparent lower cost of a centralized library service in terms of staff and equipment is often countered by the provision of separate subject areas in the care of subject librarians within the central building.

2. **Staff.** By virtue of the branch librarian's contact with the subject material, a more valuable and informed service becomes available. However, the provision of subject librarians in the central library may negate this argument.

3. **Efficiency.** A central library for a large institution cannot be other than a large building, with many sections and considerable distances between remote points. It may be more efficient for staff and students to use a smaller well-known collection located close by.

4. **Accessibility.** The size of the campus and distances to be traversed from faculty buildings to the central library are factors that should be considered. It is impossible for busy academics to make the best use of materials when they are housed in a building distant from theirs. Materials relating to special subjects are most accessible when located near the places of departmental instruction and research.[11]

5. **Interdisciplinary approach.** Computerized catalogues allow users to browse easily, and they may directly access databases much larger than their own university's through the advent of local and national networking. Woodsworth[12] believes that "providing access to the larger world of information is probably a more important issue in today's

interdisciplinary and decentralized world than is the question of where a book is housed." Hibbard[13] concurs with this statement: "When all researchers have terminals in their offices through which they can access not only their own libraries but the holdings of every major research library in the country, the question of the physical location of holdings will loose its meaning for most purposes."

6. **Communication.** For many decades communication has been raised as a valid argument in favor of centralization. However, the tools are available today to dispel the isolation of remote collections, alleviate inconvenience to users, and provide faster communication between the various disciplines. Computerized catalogues and online access to them are playing an important role in this respect.

7. **Convenience.** It is not immediately obvious why a large, centralized collection spread over many square meters of floor space in a multistoried building is more convenient than a series of well thought out topical collections housed in branch libraries. In either case a good deal of walking may be required of the researcher.[14] There is no doubt that the patrons of libraries prefer the smaller, more focused units of library service located close to their offices, laboratories, and lecture theaters.

8. **Attitudes and educational significance.** The identification of students with their specialities is furthered by a branch library. Students, particularly those in professional fields (e.g. law, engineering, medicine), may value opportunities for the creation of professional consciousness as a result of working together in a common location separate from the general student population.

9. **Technology.** Although certain services cannot be practically duplicated in a branch library system, technology has done much to increase the efficiency and reduce the isolation of the subject collection. Online union catalogues and circulation systems may easily be made available at all service points.

10. **Administrative control.** Although administrative control is better in a central library, there is far more academic interest in the affairs of the specialized library. As long as this situation is not permitted to develop into "faculty control," it can have a positive effect on a library, its collection, and its services.

11. **Adequacy.** To make a library collection complete and workable requires a measure of attention that cannot be given by a central administration that has too many interests to observe.[15] Again, this argument is countered by the provision of subject specialist librarians in a central library.

It may be seen from the above that the same criteria may be used to prove a point by both the centralist and the decentralist. The challenge for academic librarians is to provide an efficient and economical library service in the understanding that the increasingly interdisciplinary nature of knowledge means a more complex campus community. There is no simple answer to the question of how much and what kind of decentralization should be permitted.

The main disadvantage of a central library is lack of accessibility for students and staff, although attempts have been made to overcome this. Greene[16] describes a system called *LENDS* (Library Extends catalogue access and New Delivery Service) in operation at the Georgia Institute of Technology, where there is a wholly centralized library service. Remote bibliographic access is provided through the distribution of microfiche copies of the catalogue to 35 academic and research departments. Library material may be requested by telephone, and items are delivered on morning and afternoon schedules to all departments by means of a battery operated cart owned by the library. Items borrowed from the library may be returned via the same delivery service.

The main disadvantage of decentralization is expensive duplication of stock and staff. There is no way of countering this problem unless the institution has a budget that will afford good service for both general and separate libraries. In today's financial climate, a multiplication of departmental collections too small to be staffed or serviced economically or requiring extensive duplication, is unnecessary and undesirable.

Some years ago the "undergraduate" library was thought to be an attractive and acceptable compromise between centralization and decentralization. The philosophy behind this was that undergraduates deserve a facility geared to their needs, as they are frequently overlooked in the research and publication interests of the university. There is no doubt that separate undergraduate libraries help to solve the space problem occurring in main libraries, but their educational efficacy is questionable.

Shoham[17] undertook a cost/preference study of the decentralization of academic library services, using the Library School at the University of California, Berkeley, as a test case. The methodology used was to analyze various categories of cost, using data obtained from library staff; to allocate a dollar value to the users' time according to status and salary; and to obtain attitudes of users by means of a questionnaire. An analysis of this data provided interesting results:

- It was clearly shown that there was some duplication, especially in labor, to the extent of about 43% of labor cost.
- Duplication of material was surprisingly low (7%), this being the result of a careful acquisition policy adhered to in this particular library system.
- Additional costs in space, equipment, and maintenance were also incurred.
- The users preferred accessibility to greater completeness of the collection, and even very modest assumptions about the value of users' time suggested that the additional costs of decentralization could be justified in terms of overall costs.

No matter how efficient a centralized library may be on the basis of costs, it cannot be effective unless it is used by those for whom it exists. Shoham's study supports this viewpoint.

There may be an optimum size of library beyond which the service becomes too complex, impersonal, and mechanized. The optimum is perhaps a unit large enough to be efficient but small enough to retain some of the informality, accessibility, and special services of the good branch library. The desired result is a compromise between an overgrown main library and an overfragmented system of subject libraries. Aucamp[18] puts the manageable size of a library at up to 500,000 volumes, and suggests that at this point a certain measure of planned decentralization might be considered. In many cases this is more realistic than centralization. It implies the establishment of large area libraries serving the subject fields in that area. Blackburn,[19] previous librarian at the University of Toronto, believed that

> if we could start from scratch to build a complex university of 25,000 students, I should try first of all to get the teaching divisions clustered in three or four groups, each group centered on a large subject division of the centrally administered library system.

Hertz[20] agrees with Blackburn, stating that library service should be on a broad subject basis reflecting the major divisions of knowledge, the principal methods of instruction, and the needs of the students and faculty. If departments are grouped in this way and receive service from a separate library, the centralist arguments on cost and interrelation are largely overcome. Unfortunately, most universities cannot start anew and are not prepared or able to undertake massive relocations of academic faculties. Muller[21] lists certain elements of an ideal pattern:

- As much centralization as is logically feasible plus decentralized units in the largest possible segments—controlled decentralization.
- Consolidation of science branch libraries into a single library to be kept open as long as possible; personalized service, computer links to relevant databases.
- Current awareness service to academic staff.
- Opposition to separate branch libraries except medicine and law.
- Compact storage for lesser-used material.
- Easy access to regional and national collections through networking.
- Campus-wide rapid delivery of library mate-

rial to academic departments, combined with quick access to central records; similarly between libraries.

- Campus planning to aim for subject groupings of instructional buildings, so that area libraries may serve broad subjects; applicable to new and developing campuses.

In conclusion, it seems that when decentralization of a university library collection is thought to be necessary, the librarian should if possible establish large branches housing collections covering subject areas as broad as possible and serving a cluster of academic departments. Library systems with existing departmental libraries are well advised to merge small units into large ones, even in the face of faculty opposition. Experience with a library unit large enough to support adequate staff, services, and collections will, one hopes, convince a reluctant faculty of the wisdom of consolidation.

THE LINEAR LIBRARY

The concept of the linear library has not been given much serious consideration, yet it cannot be ignored if one is to examine fully the subject of centralization/decentralization. The basic concept is that while the library's administration and main services are centralized, a library continuum or "spine" reaches out to place the bookstock as close as possible to teaching departments.[22]

The principle has been used at the University of Bielefeld (Federal Republic of Germany), the University of Cape Town (South Africa), the New University of Ulster (Northern Ireland), and the University of Odense (Denmark). It was considered for the University of Jos in Nigeria, but the idea was discarded in favor of a central library. No further mention of linear or spine libraries has been traced in the literature. Although theoretically the linear library should provide maximum service to readers at reduced cost, and a logical answer to the problem of decentralization while preserving control, in practice the concept is not favored. The following is a brief description of Bielefeld University Library

and its underlying philosophy, which will illustrate the linear principle.

BIELEFELD UNIVERSITY LIBRARY

The University of Bielefeld was established in 1969 as a result of public demand for a university in Westphalia, West Germany. It is unlike other universities in that with the exception of a few subordinate structures and a large parking garage, it consists of one enormous building, an integral unit with flexible interior design. A large, two-story central hall is bordered by two parallel buildings of concrete and glass rising to eight and nine floors respectively, and the central axis serves as a connecting passage, permitting access to all divisions. The plan of this main building is a variation of the "comb" scheme, with individual blocks arranged on both sides of the central passage. From the exterior a broad stairway (essential due to the sloping site) leads from the main entrance to the central hall. From here a peripheral gallery at mezzanine level provides access to the reading rooms of the library, which occupies the entire first floor.

The library has central administrative offices, an interlibrary loans department, general reference collection, and technical processing section. These are housed on three floors of the building (1st basement, ground, and 1st level). The reading and bookstack areas are divided among five separate spaces that house three science and seven humanities collections. Offices of the various subject librarians are located in these spaces.

There is no real main entrance to the library. Entry to any branch reading room north or south of the longitudinal axis of the hall provides access to all other reading rooms, which together form a spatial continuum (see Fig. 7.1). In three cases—literature, sociology, and history—the floor below is also included in this continuum.[23] The teaching departments with their administrative offices, seminar rooms, laboratories, and lecture theaters are housed on floors above and below the reading rooms.

The library as a whole provides seating for 2,675 readers and houses a bookstock of approximately 1 million items (with a capacity of over 2

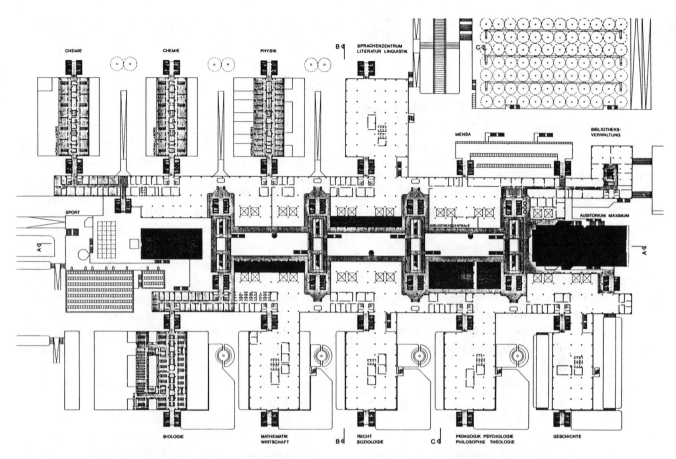

Fig. 7.1. Bielefeld University Library: Floor Plan. *Source:* "Universität Bielefeld: Planungsablauf." Bielefeld, 1976. By permission from Harro Heim, retired Director of Library Services, Bielefeld University.

million). It covers an area of 139,387 m² (1,500,360 ft²). The branch libraries include reading areas, open access bookstacks, special work areas, microfiche and online catalogues, reference collections, and audiovisual materials, as well as the necessary personnel and administrative space (see Fig. 7.2).

Regarding communications, there are passenger and goods elevators from the entrance to the reading rooms in each block. In addition, reading rooms occupying two floors contain book elevators. As a result of financial restrictions during construction, no further transport facilities are provided.[24] However, modern data processing techniques have proved to be a vital and positive factor in promoting administrative cohesion and in integrating the library system. Circulation systems at all access points are automated, and ordering and cataloguing of material are done online. Thus information on the avail-

ability of material is at the disposal of the user at any point in the system.

The fundamental principles determining the structure of the library have been outlined by Krieg:[25]

- The information centers were to be linked to the library's central administrative and technical services.
- They were to be administered by qualified staff responsible to the librarian.
- Materials were to be on open access.
- The faculties themselves were to participate in the acquisition of material for each respective library.

Thus the system, described by the Bielefeld Foundation Committee as "a radical solution to the concept of decentralization," allows each of the university institutes sufficient scope to influ-

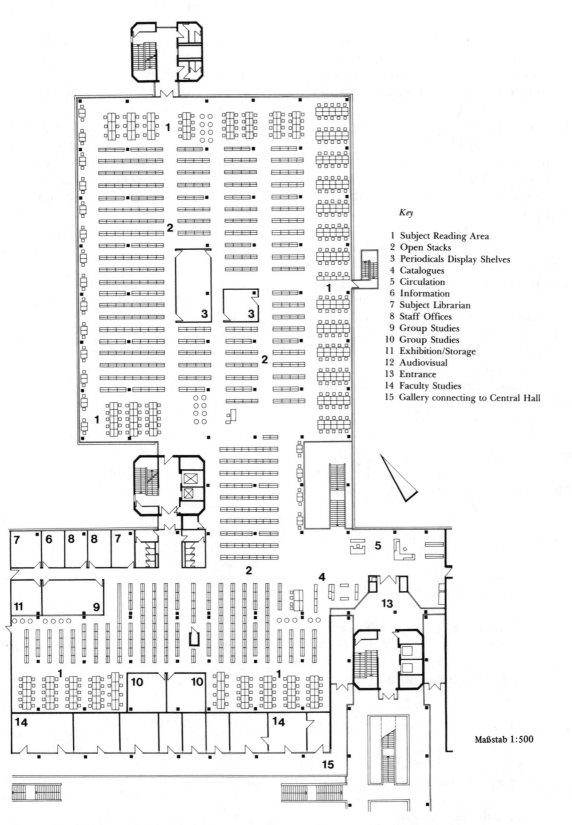

Key

1 Subject Reading Area
2 Open Stacks
3 Periodicals Display Shelves
4 Catalogues
5 Circulation
6 Information
7 Subject Librarian
8 Staff Offices
9 Group Studies
10 Group Studies
11 Exhibition/Storage
12 Audiovisual
13 Entrance
14 Faculty Studies
15 Gallery connecting to Central Hall

Maßstab 1:500

Fig. 7.2. Bielefeld University: Typical Branch Library. *Source:* Rolf Fuhlrott, Gerhard Liebers, and Franz-Heinrich Philipp, *Bibliotheksneubauten in der Bundesrepublik Deutschland, 1968–1983.* Frankfurt am Main: Vittorio Klostermann, 1983, p. 22. By permission from Vittorio Klostermann.

ence the development of its library in accordance with its specific research requirements.[26]

It was felt to be necessary, however, to keep the number of branch libraries to a minimum by integrating the customary institute libraries into larger units; to regard the university library as a single unit; to guard against book collections being built up erratically without sufficient consideration being given to future research needs; and to ensure that the authority of the library staff was not reduced.

Heim,[27] director of the University of Bielefeld Library until October 1984, reports that the concept and structure of the library has endured several crucial test situations over the past eight years. In its early years only the circulation system was computerized. The introduction of automated acquisition and cataloguing functions was delayed for a considerable time. This lack of system information in turn delayed user acceptance of the linear library principle. The importance of online information at each inquiry/circulation point in the system cannot be overemphasized. If unavailable, the problem of fast communication over considerable distances is almost insurmountable. In conclusion, it is possible that a linear library may operate adequately when:

- the university is planned in its entirety from the beginning and the library is taken into account in these early stages;
- the branches are viable book collections in themselves;
- sufficient thought and finance is expended on excellent communication systems, both in terms of horizontal and vertical transportation and electronic links between all parts of the system.

Dangers are that:

- if branches are to be accessible to user departments, there will of necessity be large distances between remote points of the system;
- this could actually *impede* access;
- it will in all likelihood encourage the duplication of stock in overlapping areas;
- the main advantage of the system—accessibil-

ity—cannot be maintained after normal working hours without expensive employment of additional staff;
- security is reduced with an increase in entrance/exit points;
- persons studying interdisciplinary subjects are at a disadvantage, as in a decentralized system;
- expansion is a very real problem unless the principle of self-renewal is applied;
- the initial logic guiding the configuration of faculty buildings is likely to become disrupted if a new faculty building is added and the spine (with the library) correspondingly extended.

Accessibility is important to the user. However, good administration, effective library management, and efficient information retrieval are also extremely important. The advantages and disadvantages of a proposed (or existing) library system must be carefully weighed in the context of the specific local environment and set of circumstances.

REFERENCES

1. J. Raffel and R. Shishko, "Centralization vs. decentralization: a location analysis approach for librarians," *Special Libraries,* vol.63, no.3, 1972, p.135.
2. Rutgers University, Graduate School of Library Science, *Studies in Library Administrative Problems: Eight Reports from a Seminar in Library Administration* (New Brunswick, N.J.: The University, 1960), p.17.
3. A.R. Wells, "Another look at centralization and decentralization of university libraries," *Libra,* no.8, 1973, pp.26–35.
4. Centralization and decentralization in academic libraries: a symposium. Papers presented at the 46th Annual Conference of Eastern College Librarians at Columbia University, 1960. Introduction by M.F. Tauber. *College and Research Libraries,* vol.22, 1961, p.327.
5. F.H. Wagman, quoted in N.O. Rush, "Central vs. departmental libraries," *Mountain Plains Library Quarterly,* vol.7, 1962.
6. J. Legg, "The death of the departmental library," *Library Resources and Technical Services,* vol.9, no.3, 1965, p.351.
7. J.M. Bruno, p.314.
8. "Centralization or decentralization of library collections: a symposium," *Journal of Academic Librarianship,* vol.9, no.4, 1983, p.197.

9. J. Legg, p.352.
10. "Centralization or decentralization of library collections," p.200.
11. R.A. Millar, "Centralization vs. decentralization," *American Library Association Bulletin*, vol.33, 1939, p.79.
12. "Centralization or decentralization of library collections," p.199.
13. Ibid., p.200.
14. Ibid., p.199.
15. R.A. Millar, p.78.
16. R.J. Greene, "*LENDS:* an approach to the centralization/decentralization dilemma," *College and Research Libraries*, vol.36, no.3, 1975, p.201.
17. S. Shoham, "A cost-preference study of the decentralization of academic library services," *Library Research*, vol.4, 1982, p.175.
18. P. Aucamp, "*Die Sentralisasie en Desentralisasie van Universiteitsbiblioteke.*" M.A. dissertation, Potchefstroom, The University, 1972, p.135.
19. R.H. Blackburn, quoted in R.H. Muller, "Master planning for university libraries," *Library Trends*, October 1969, p.144.
20. G. Hertz, quoted in A.M. McAnnaly, "Departments in university libraries," *Library Trends*, vol.7, 1959, p.459.
21. R.H. Muller, "Master planning for university libraries," *Library Trends*, October 1969, pp.147–48.
22. University of Cape Town Libraries, *The Linear Library Moves Towards Completion* (Cape Town: The University Libraries, 1983), p.2.
23. R. Fuhlrott et al., *Bibliotheksneubauten in der Bundesrepublik Deutschland, 1968–1983* (Frankfurt am Main: Vittorio Klosterman, 1983), p.16.
24. Ibid., p.17.
25. W. Krieg and J. Stoltzenburg, "Zentralisierung und Dezentralisierung im Entwurf und Gegenentwurf für ein Bibliothekssystem der Universität Bielefeld: *Verband der Bibliotheken des Landes Nordheim—Westfalen Mitteilungsblatt*," *Neue Folge*, vol.18, no.2, 1968, p.96.
26. Ibid.
27. Personal communication received from Harro Heim, director of the University of Bielefeld Library, May 1984.

8   *Planning for the New Technology*

Automation may be defined as "the use of machinery to save mental and manual effort" (*Concise Oxford Dictionary,* 5th ed., 1964). In any library one will find automatic equipment that is taken completely for granted—photocopiers, calculators, electronic book security systems, and typewriters. More recently the computer has made an impact on libraries worldwide, with computer technology interacting to a large degree in the daily work of librarians. The new technology is able to produce and disseminate information in a variety of forms and at great speed. In its own way, the electronic revolution is having as great an effect on the availability of information as Gutenberg's invention of movable type nearly five centuries ago. In most academic libraries today the computer has become indispensable in the operation of effective library systems.

It is not my intention to review types of information systems nor to assess the impact of electronic communication on our society. On the assumption, however, that libraries must inevitably become more and more involved with this technology if they are to remain serious contenders in the information market, consideration will be given to some of the possible effects of these developments on libraries from a physical planning point of view. Planners must be confident that the buildings they plan today will be usable tomorrow. They should keep in mind that the libraries of the future will have to be more "information-outgoing."[1]

Computers have been used in libraries for three major purposes: (a) to automate internal record-keeping systems; (b) to ascertain what information exists in the library and whether it is currently available; (c) to permit access to information not physically present in the library, i.e. information located within a network area, state or country, or available in other countries via commercial databases. This third function is extremely important. It alters one's whole traditional concept of a library from a collection of physical objects to a vast store of information in intangible electronic form.[2] The results of the new technology are many and varied—electronic publishing, computer storage of vast amounts of information, quick and easy retrieval of this information, networking, more efficient "housekeeping" systems, and sophisticated document delivery. What effect these will ultimately have on libraries is a debatable point. It is possible that central or large main libraries will grow even larger, offering more services to users. Rohlf,[3] however, predicts that branch libraries could possibly decrease in physical size because of the possibilities of remote bibliographic access, computer links to numerous files in the central library, and a numerical reduction in the serial holdings necessary at multiple points. Libraries should be able to send services out to academic departments in the form of bibliographic information, following up with the actual items supplied by the main library or a large branch.

> The present surge of students to the library for concentrated, disciplined study, especially at times of academic pressure, is however unlikely to be reduced by technology. . . . Generally the more that technology facilitates access to information, the more will information and libraries be used, which will tend to increase, not reduce, library workloads and the size of library facilities.[4]

Given these service conditions, there will be various environmental and design problems to be considered. Some computer hardware requires certain preconditions which if not provided could have a direct effect on future operations. Libraries today make use of mainframe, mini-, or microcomputers, or a combination of these, in order to operate various computerized systems and to obtain information from various sources. A mainframe computer is generally the responsibility of the parent institution; the library uses it, but does not have to house it. Mini- and microcomputers are much more frequently located in libraries. Minicomputers are just as efficient as mainframe computers as far as speed is concerned, but usually cannot handle such a wide range of applications. Initially they tended to be used for specific jobs requiring little program alteration, but nowadays are much more flexible and are used in a variety of configurations. As a stand-alone system, the minicomputer offers the library a computer system that may effectively be under its own control, thus doing away with problems of low priority and low accessibility so often associated with library use of a mainframe. Unless the installation is unusually large, it requires a relatively small space on a desk top, with no special environmental conditions.

Microcomputers generally comprise a microprocessor, a keyboard, a visual display unit, and a cassette tape recorder for secondary storage. There are several potential areas of application in libraries, but they are of no use where large volumes of data must be stored and accessed.

When installing a computer, there are two aspects to be considered: the console and the terminals. The console houses the computer and peripheral devices such as disc drives for information storage, tape drives for record conversions, and a variety of printers. The terminals are linked to the console via the data cables and are located in preselected areas throughout the library.

SPACE

The space requirements for the console will vary depending on the size of the system. Mainframes are large; minicomputers are much smaller and do not generally occupy more than 12 m^2 (130 ft^2) of space. There should be 1 m free on all sides of the system to permit engineers access during installation and for servicing. This will also allow adequate air flow around the equipment.[5] As libraries grow, so too will storage requirements, and it is advisable to plan for additional storage devices at the time of the initial installation. Space should also be provided to store disc packs, magnetic tapes, data processing forms, and supplies such as overdue notices, form letters, and other user documentation. Most computer equipment is becoming progressively smaller, with fewer technical and environmental requirements. Thus although library planners should provide for a computer room to house such equipment and its associated functions, they should ensure that this space be flexible.

SECURITY AND SITING

In all cases where a computer is housed within a library, security should be taken into consideration. It is preferable to place computer equipment in a lockable room, usually in a windowless and controlled area of the building. Direct sunlight should be avoided as this can cause heat build-up which can affect data storage and light-sensitive switching devices. It should not be located close to any radio frequency-generating equipment such as radiograms, television receivers and high-fidelity systems. Some electronic equipment emits signals that can interfere with the operation of a sensitive central processing unit (CPU), and in some cases even a photocopier may cause interference.[6]

POWER

Power requirements are specified by the manufacturer of the system. Power is a critical factor, especially when a new line is run into an old building. In certain circumstances the power supply may not be stable enough for computing equipment due to fluctuation, and there may be a need for a constant voltage transformer to regulate it. Surges in power cause errors in the data and can damage the equipment, resulting in poor performance and excessive downtime. Therefore a dedicated circuit is recommended—a line straight from the main power box in the building that does not have any other equipment of any sort attached to it. Facility for expansion should be built-in if a second phase, possibly requiring an additional disc storage unit, is envisaged. An extra dedicated line will eliminate the need for further electrical work at a later stage. Conventional wall outlets are also required, placed close to the system. These will be needed by service and maintenance personnel for their test equipment. To facilitate the use of terminals throughout the building, a flexible system of electrical and coaxial conduiting must be provided both vertically between floors and horizontally on each floor.[7]

Environmental Considerations

Although larger CPUs may require a more strictly controlled environment than smaller ones, in most cases temperature, humidity, dust, noise, and lighting should be taken into consideration.

1. **Temperature.** Fortunately the temperature range in which computers operate best is comparable to that for humans—18°C to 29°C (64°F to 84°F). When the temperature rises above the upper limit, equipment failures may occur that can reduce the life expectancy of the equipment. Computers dissipate heat, measured in British thermal units (BTUs), in proportion to their size. The manufacturer can provide the BTU/hour measure for each piece of equipment, and an air conditioning expert may then calculate the air conditioning capacity required. The system itself, the number of people in the room, the location of windows (if any), and the degree of sunlight entering the room are all factors that must be considered. A raised computer floor with space for air conditioning ducts piped directly into machines could be a requirement, while smaller computers may

require only room air conditioning.[8] Because the size of computers is constantly decreasing, it is frequently found that the latter is sufficient.

2. **Humidity.** In very humid areas it may be necessary to dehumidify the air, while in dry areas, it may be necessary to add moisture. In the latter areas, if this is not done, a build-up of static electricity could have an adverse effect on the computer. A humidity level in the region of 50% is suitable.[9]
3. **Dust.** Incoming air should be dust-free. Dust may be harmful, especially if it gets into the electro-mechanical storage devices of the CPU. The room containing the CPU should be kept as clean as possible, and preferably should have a higher air pressure than surrounding areas to prevent dust from seeping in under doors.
4. **Noise.** Some equipment is noisy and will require isolation if it is to be installed in an otherwise quiet library environment. If possible, acoustic ceiling or wall tiles should be used to absorb sound.
5. **Lighting.** Lighting in the computer room is not usually a critical factor. If it is comfortable for those working there, this is adequate for the installation.

Building Requirements

Library planners should consider access. If inadequate, the size of doorways, elevators, and staircases can pose formidable problems when a system is being installed. A vehicle delivery area is also very useful.

One of the most important considerations for library planning today is that of ducting, either under the floor or contained in false ceilings, installed when the building is under construction. In the past electrical conduits (¾ inch or 20 mm pipe or flexible tubing) were used to carry the electrical cables. Today most libraries being planned and built have a three-duct system. Each duct is approximately 75 mm wide and 50 mm deep (3ins × 2ins), although this size may vary considerably. One is used for telephone cabling, the other for electrical cable, and the

A. *System Delivery Considerations*
   1. Can the receiving area handle the following?
      - weight of system
      - dimensions of largest carton
   2. Is there a receiving dock at the level of a truck bed?
   3. Are doorways, hallways and elevators wide enough to accommodate the system?
   4. If there is no elevator, will the system have to be carried upstairs?
   5. Is there a convenient place to store the equipment until it can be installed?
   6. Will library personnel be available to help in moving the system?
B. *Building and Space Considerations*
   1. Is there sufficient space for the following items?
      - all main unit components
      - work area for servicing the components
      - future expansion
      - storage area near the main unit components
   2. Is there space arranged for terminals, display stations, charging stations and appropriate work areas around each type of terminal?
C. *Temperature Conditions*
   1. Is there sufficient air conditioning within the room where the main unit will be located to maintain the temperature in the range of 65°–85° with a variance of less than 10°?
D. *Antistatic Consideration*
   1. Can humidity in the range of 40–80% be maintained?
   2. Has use of the following measures to reduce the effects of static electricity been discussed with the vendor?
      - maintaining the humidity level
      - laying antistatic mats under the main unit
      - spraying antistatic spray on the carpet
      - not waxing the floors
      - not using steel brushes to clean the floor
E. *Electrical Considerations*
   1. Have the following arrangements for main unit electrical circuits and connectors been made?
      - . . . AMP dedicated circuit for the main unit
      - separate circuit breaker for the main unit
      - separate . . . AMP for each disk drive
      - separate 15 AMP circuit for each fast printer
      - separate 15 AMP circuit for each magnetic tape unit
      - separate circuitry as necessary for any other equipment
   2. Have the following arrangements for terminal connections been made?
      - connection to a 20 AMP circuit for each display terminal
      - connection to a 20 AMP circuit for each hardcopy terminal
      - 3-conducted shielded cable for each local terminal
      - individual connections for light pens or laser scanners as necessary
F. *Telephone Consideration*
   1. Have arrangements been made for the following?
      - one telephone within five feet of the main unit
      - one dedicated line for each dial-up terminal with answering device at each end if necessary
G. *Supplies*
   1. Have arrangements been made for paper supplies not provided by the vendor?
      - paper for main unit printer(s)
      - paper for notices
      - paper for display terminals

Fig. 8.1. Checklist for Computer Installation. *Source:* Barbara G. Toohill, "Guide to Library Automation." McLean, Va.: MITRE Corporation, 1980, p. 107. By permission from Barbara G. Toohill, Group Leader, AI Systems Planning, MITRE Corporation. Reprinted in ERIC Reports, p. 107 (overstamped 102). Washington, D.C.: U.S. Department of Health, Education and Welfare, 1980.

third for low-voltage requirements or for signaling controls. This third duct is becoming essential in modern library planning, because it carries the coaxial cables for the computer equipment, and running alongside the telephone duct, gives online accessibility. In some buildings ducts have been spaced as close as 1 m (3ft) on centers, but this is very costly. Obviously the closer the ducts, the greater the flexibility, but in many instances wider spacing of, say, 3 m (10ft) is perfectly adequate. Spacing is a question that must be resolved for each individual building.[10]

The location of cables as well as wall power outlets may limit or dictate the location of terminals within the library. Terminals at remote locations (e.g. branch libraries) or those not directly connected by data cable to the computer will need to be linked to the system by telephone lines. They will also require wall outlets for power.

Fire precautions are important. The computer room should be noncombustible, including walls, floor, and ceiling. Portable fire extinguishers are advisable, and an automatic fire control system is recommended for larger rooms. Halon gas systems appear to be particularly effective.[11] Staff should be trained to operate the emergency power-off system, whereby all equipment can be shut down simultaneously should a problem occur.

TERMINALS

The major consideration is space. Most will require approximately 0.4 m² (4.3 ft²) with additional space for those operating in conjunction with light pens or similar equipment (see Fig. 8.2). Adequate space around the terminal is necessary for books and documentation. Environmental requirements are not too restrictive, the main one being lighting: If a terminal is wrongly located, reflection on the screen may cause eye strain on the part of the user. Light intensity should be below 70 foot-candles,[12] as illumination above this level will tend to bleach out the image on the screen. With illumination engineers recommending light intensity levels of 150 and even 200 foot-candles in reading areas, careful consideration must be given to this prob-

Fig. 8.2. Computerized Circulation Using an Optical Laser Scanner (University of Witwatersrand Library, Johannesburg)

lem. If static electricity becomes a problem in dry climates, equipment should be placed on antistatic mats, or antistatic spray may be used.

HUMAN FACTORS

Many mini- and microcomputer systems advertise that they do not require special installation except for the addition of electric and telephone lines.[13] To run the system this may be true, but the purchase of a computer system subtly changes the library. It is likely to become more service-oriented. Revised layout may become necessary to effect good work flow. In addition, terminals require a different kind of work station. If one considers automation of library functions, one must consider the idea of librarians working in an environment where information is generated, organized, indexed, stored, transferred, selected, retrieved, or discarded at the push of a few buttons. The speed with which an error may be compounded is hard to imagine. It is thus very important that the work station should help to prevent possible errors by being well designed and comfortable and by being correctly placed in terms of work flow. Experience has shown that when automation is attempted without understanding the requirements of the people it is supposed to help, results can be disastrous. Ergonomics, or human factor engineering, is not a new science, but its relevance to the library profession is only now being appreciated. Pinder and Storey[14] suggest that libraries have tended to neglect the human factor because of two handicaps: "a plethora of old buildings and a lack of new money." It costs so much merely to install the new technology that there is insufficient funding left over to give consideration to the working environment.

Space requirements for members of the library staff increase as terminals, modems, printers, and personal computers become standard items of equipment. As Beckman[15] points out, space is critical particularly in the transitional period from manual to automated systems, when typewriter and terminal both occupy space on a library assistant's desk, and when cataloguers need terminals in addition to their customary

tools. The standard 110 ft^2 (± 10 m^2) per staff member will be inadequate in the computerized library. The office environment should be designed so that staff may work comfortably, and the workstation should be designed to fit the specific task. Desks, chairs, and document holders should be designed around the operator, and adjustability is an essential requirement where the workstation is used by a number of people. Features worth noting are:[16]

- large surfaces to cater for all user needs;
- plentiful power sources and short cables;
- working height high enough to avoid cramped legs, and low enough to have keyboard at elbow height;
- seat height and tilt and backrest height and tilt all fully adjustable;
- document holders at same level and viewing distance as the screen to minimize head and body movement.

The surrounding environment should not be neglected either.[17] Glare may be a problem, and staff should face away from windows or other sources of light. The terminal should ideally be located between light fixtures so that they are not parallel to the screen, and fluorescent tubes should be fitted with diffusers. In most cases the fluorescent lighting provided in libraries is too bright for working at a terminal. One can tell how much reflection there is merely by looking at the screen when the video display unit is turned off.

To rest the eyes from the strain of looking at the screen, care should be taken that surrounding walls and ceilings do not reflect glare. Items such as pictures, posters, and indoor plants can also assist in resting the eyes from the screen.

As libraries begin to make use of terminals in public areas for the use of patrons, there will in all likelihood be some user resistance to the new technology. Increased emphasis on the development of "user-friendly" terminals will result, because the use of a terminal is either pleasant or unpleasant depending on the confidence users feel in their own abilities. Mooers[18] states that "an information retrieval system will tend not to be used whenever it is more painful and troublesome for a customer to have information than for him not to have it." As much care as possible should be taken that library users as well as library staff find the equipment simple to operate and unintimidating.

People using electronic equipment will require more sophisticated facilities such as individual carrels supplied with both electrical and coaxial cabling and with sufficient space to hold viewing equipment.[19] It is obvious that more space will become necessary as each reader station acquires a more sophisticated environment. A standard for user space allocation of 30–35 ft^2 (2.8–3.3 m^2), rather than the present 25 ft^2 (2.3 m^2), would appear reasonable. In addition, more individual reader stations are likely to be required, rather than the 2-, 4-, and 8-place tables frequently found in libraries. A new look at the provision of user facilities is required. As library patrons become more familiar with technology and it becomes an integral part of their library experience, they will expect to find it easily accessible and available throughout the library, not just in one location[20] (examples are online catalogues, microform reader-printers, photocopiers).

It may be seen from the above that numerous site preparation factors may need to be considered before introducing computerized systems. Toohill[21] has compiled a checklist that summarizes these factors and is a useful guide to librarians (see Fig. 8.1).

REFERENCES

1. R.H. Rohlf, "Building-planning implications of automation," *in* American Library Association, Information Science and Automation Division, *Library Automation: A State of the Art Review*. Papers presented at the Preconference Institute on Library Automation, ed. S.R. Salmon (Chicago: ALA, 1969), p.33.
2. F.W. Lancaster, "The paperless society revisited," *American Libraries,* September 1985, p.554.
3. R.H. Rohlf, p.34.
4. Education Facilities Laboratories, *The Impact of Technology on the Library Building* (New York: EFL, 1967), p.18.
5. R.P. Stroum, "Physical planning for automated circulation systems," *Library Journal Special Report No.4*, p.12.
6. Elaine Cohen and Aaron Cohen, *Automation, Space Management and Productivity: A Guide for Libraries* (New York: Bowker, 1981), p.60.
7. Education Facilities Laboratories, p.17.
8. Cohen, p.56.
9. Ibid., p.61.
10. Rohlf, p.35.
11. Cohen, p.62.
12. Education Facilities Laboratories, p.19.
13. Cohen, p.67.
14. C. Pinder and C. Storey, "Green light for new technology?" *Library Association Record,* vol.88, no.6, 1986, p.282.
15. M. Beckman, "Library buildings in the network environment," *Journal of Academic Librarianship,* vol.9, no.5, p.283.
16. Pinder, p.282.
17. Ibid.
18. M.E.D. Koenig, "The convergence of Moore's/Mooers' laws," *Information Processing and Management,* vol.23, no.6, 1987, p.583.
19. Beckman.
20. Ibid.
21. B.G. Toohill, *Guide to Library Automation* (Washington, D.C.: U.S. Department of Health, Education, and Welfare, National Institute of Education, ERIC Reports, 1980).

9 *Planning for Audiovisual Developments*

Educators today are becoming increasingly concerned about the way in which students are taught, and are beginning to make use of all available means of communication in the process of instruction. Many teachers use audiovisual aids to augment lectures. Others permit students to listen to tape recordings or watch videocassettes instead of attending classes. Some are interested in producing their own instructional materials such as tape/slide programs and video recordings that allow students to study at their own pace. Foreign language courses regularly employ language laboratories. Interactive video is starting to make its presence felt. Young people are constantly exposed to a variety of media such as transistor radios, record players, television sets, videocassette recorders, and, more recently, computers. Many school systems use educational technology, and as more students are exposed to this type of environment, it is inevitable that educational changes will take place at the university level.[1]

Although the academic library is being drawn into these developments, the response on the part of librarians is not always enthusiastic. The high cost of hardware and facilities, of staff, and of training these staff members as media specialists has dampened enthusiasm in many cases. Funding is a crucial element in the development of a successful media center. Over and above implementation of the facility is the high cost of maintaining, replacing, and updating media materials and equipment and the need to experiment with the new technology. Adequate and regular budgetary support is essential, even though this intrudes upon already limited book and staffing budgets.[2] Other problems are the difficulties in servicing equipment; of providing backup systems for those items that are being repaired, have missing parts, or have been stolen; and the incompatibility of systems. Despite these difficulties, university librarians should be careful not to distance themselves from the instructional process. They are involved in higher education, and should provide for the teaching needs of the university, whatever the format. They should be tackling with enthusiasm, not suspicion, the task of building up a worthwhile audiovisual center and of "selling" its services to staff and students alike. With the growth of distance learning, self-paced learning, individualized learning, and the need to continue to learn throughout one's lifetime as career patterns change, the roles of teacher and librarian merge toward the common goal of knowledge transmission. The combination of the librarian, teacher, and information and audiovisual technology can provide a formidable force in the learning process.[3]

My purpose in this chapter is not to discuss the learning resources center as such, but rather to look at the traditional book-oriented academic library into which nonprint materials are being increasingly integrated. The special preparation of areas for the use of these materials is essential, and planners and architects should give careful consideration to:

- learning spaces for individual students and different sized groups of students;
- spaces for the production (possibly), maintenance, and storage of equipment and materials;
- spaces for staff and administrative functions.

A number of questions should be asked when planning these facilities:[4]

- What will students be doing in these areas?
- What are their needs?
- What size groups and for how long will students be using the facilities?
- What is the size of the physical facility required?
- What is the budget for developing the facility?
- What hardware and software will be placed here? (storage, open-access, and display requirements).
- What architectural and technical needs must be considered?

Planners may benefit greatly by involving the users themselves in the planning process. Faculty can provide useful information on the ways in which they could make use of the center, what numbers of students or size of groups they envisage will use the resources, and what the demand on facilities is likely to be. Students themselves are always happy to try out and assess different types of furniture and equipment, and are generally fairly outspoken in expressing their opinions.

ENVIRONMENTAL FACTORS

Environmental factors are important in the preservation of audiovisual material. Wall[5] has investigated the effects of various environmental conditions on different types of material and concludes (fortunately) that temperatures most suitable for humans—16 to 21°C (60 to 70°F)—are also most suitable for various media formats such as videotape, magnetic tape, and floppy disc, with 18°C (65°F) being the optimum. "Whatever temperature is decided upon, it is important that it remain as constant as possible, as fluctuation can harm materials." Relative humidity may also have an adverse effect. Wall suggests that a humidity level of 45% (±5%) is considered suitable, with 47% as the optimum. Excessive humidity may cause metal items to rust, tapes may become abrasive, and films may develop mold and fungus. Lack of humidity may cause materials to become brittle.

Audiovisual materials should be housed in an environment as dust-free as possible. Dust coats films, tapes, and lenses, and may be ground into the materials as they are used, causing poor reproduction and scratches.[6] When not in use, all software should be kept covered, and a regular cleaning routine established for all equipment. Air-conditioning units with air filtration systems effective against dust particles are ideal. In industrial areas, air washers may be necessary. A further environmental factor of which planners should be aware is the detrimental effect of sunlight—both the ultraviolet rays of the sun and the possible heat build-up in areas close to windows. Many audiovisual materials exposed to direct sunlight will be ruined.[7]

The existence of magnetic fields may also create problems. Information stored on magnetic tape or housed in electromagnetic storage devices is particularly sensitive to magnets, electric motors, transformers, and certain security devices, and proximity to such machines may cause loss of data and tape breakage.[8]

FLEXIBILITY

This is of utmost importance when attempting to accommodate varying numbers of students and types of material and equipment with a limited budget. Flexible arrangements will require movable furniture and fittings, which are likely to include chairs, tables, screens (for projection), screens (for dividing up spaces), equipment trolleys, whiteboards, and display boards. An adaptable space will easily facilitate the growth in use of one kind of material, decline in the use of another, an increase in the amount of equipment required, or the replacement of that equipment with up-to-date models. Wherever feasible, spaces for large groups should be capable of division into smaller spaces through the use of mobile partitions or "concertina" doors.

POWER

The ideal power supply for a media center (and indeed for the whole library) is contained in a cable system under the floor, installed at the time of construction, with ducting between 1 m and

3 m (3 ft and 10 ft) on centers. Although this provides the necessary flexibility as regards location of equipment, type of equipment, and power loading, it is expensive to install, and many library planners have had to compromise by providing ducting around the perimeter of the area. Outlets at building columns should always be available as study stations containing equipment can often be located advantageously near such columns. If facilities are needed in open areas, the "power column" may be used. This is a pole that extends from floor to ceiling where power is available. Although unattractive and a traffic hazard, these are flexible, inexpensive, and have much to recommend them.[9] As many power sockets as possible should be provided—somehow there are never enough. For safety reasons, all sockets should be flush with the surface and have individual switches. Those located at table height are particularly convenient. It should be easy to insert or remove plugs without having to bend them or pull on the wires, as this can be dangerous, and wires trailing over the floor should be avoided at all costs.[10] Library planners must ensure that the electrical circuitry will be able to carry the maximum possible load envisaged given that many items of equipment will be used simultaneously. Many libraries, planned and constructed with flexibility and future requirements in mind, have required additional circuits several years later as excessive loading caused existing power supplies to "trip out." The acquisition of electrical and electronic equipment in academic libraries has developed more rapidly than many libraries thought possible, and there is every reason to believe that this trend will continue. Those involved in planning today should therefore make very generous provision for power supply.

LIGHTING

Lighting systems need to be suitable for all the activities that occur in the audiovisual center, and these should be identified at the planning stage. They may include note taking and discussion; projection of slides, films, and overhead transparencies; viewing of television or computer terminal screens; and displays of various kinds. Appropriate levels of illumination on screen and display surfaces, work surfaces, and surroundings need to be considered, with a suitable means of controlling these levels of artificial lighting as well as natural light sources. It is advisable to have wall light switches with dimmers located at both the front and back of the viewing area for the convenience of lecturers and operators. For projection purposes lights should run parallel to the front of the room, not toward the screen. If this is not possible, a combination of incandescent lighting at the back and fluorescent lighting in the front is recommended; the fluorescent lights may then be switched off for viewing purposes. In order to obtain the best image it should be possible to lower the level of light in audiovisual areas to $\frac{1}{10}$ foot-candle.[11] When using television sets or monitors, care must be taken that lighting is not too bright, and reflections on the screen should be avoided. The ambient light should ideally be at a similar brightness to that of the screen so as to reduce any potential eyestrain.[12] Natural light may be blocked in a number of ways:[13]

- Opaque shades, held within a metal track, which prevent light from entering. If tracks are not available, shades one size larger than the windows, providing an overlap area, are very effective.
- Opaque curtains, which should extend below the bottom of the window. Weighted hems add to their effectiveness.
- Venetian blinds.

These controls are recommended for front or rear projection onto screens. However, total blackout facilities are not normally necessary for much of the modern viewing hardware available today, which is designed for successful operation in normally lit rooms with no loss in viewing quality.[14]

ACOUSTICS

Acoustic considerations include the distribution of sound within the space, the passage of sound between spaces, and levels of background noise.

Because there may be a high degree of movement and considerable noise within an audiovisual center, it is necessary to plan for the acoustic difficulties that will be encountered. Curtains, soft floor coverings, and sound-absorbing screens will be useful for this purpose, and some areas may be improved by carpeting the back wall. Most media hardware operates relatively quietly, and carpeting and curtaining will absorb any motor noise generated. Media operating in open areas should be used with headphones, and these should be of a sufficiently high quality to prevent sound from carrying into surrounding spaces. Noisier machines should be relegated to closed rooms or separate areas.

FURNISHINGS

Students may spend long periods of time in the audiovisual area. Thus every effort should be made to create a pleasant and visually attractive environment. Whether part of a new library, an addition to an existing plant, or renovated space, attention should be given to the proportions of the main areas of the audiovisual center to avoid long, narrow, low-ceilinged spaces that are undesirable from both the aesthetic and functional standpoint. Selection of paint colors, furnishings, and materials for floors, walls, and ceilings should be coordinated to produce harmonious surroundings in which environmental control (temperature and humidity), lighting, acoustics, and maintenance factors have all been given proper attention.

In a study of the interaction of people with their environment, Sommer[15] concludes that environment has an influence on teaching and learning. Studies of libraries show that a strong relationship exists between layout, perception of activity, student characteristics, interaction patterns, and use of space. This suggests that planners ought to give close attention to each of these variables. What takes place within these learning spaces is a highly complex psychological, sociological, and physical interaction that will affect a student's ability to concentrate and retain information. Functional, aesthetic, and ergonomic criteria should be established in the planning stages.

Seating may be fixed, movable, or a combination of both. Fixed seating has the advantage of ensuring that every occupant is in the proper relationship to display surfaces and screens, but limits flexibility and is possibly only appropriate in a lecture theater or small auditorium located within the library. Movable seating permits flexibility in arranging rooms to meet particular requirements. Some commercially available seats have their own tablet arms for writing, but these arms are often far too small for student needs. Where movable seating is provided, it is preferable to have a flexible arrangement of tables which may be used for seminar or discussion groups. Trapezium tables are particularly adaptable in this respect. Movable screens are useful to break up larger rooms into smaller work areas, and these may also be used as display surfaces or projection screens.

Six main factors may be identified in the process of furniture selection:[16,17]

1. **Design.** Furniture should be selected that suits the architecture of the building and the atmosphere to be conveyed. It should be functional first of all. This relates to comfort, convenience, efficiency of operation, and serviceability. Much can be achieved with a combination of design, fabric texture, and color. Materials in furniture are selected for their characteristics of beauty, versatility, strength, resistance to wear, to dirt, adaptability, and cost. The finish should protect the surface of the material and enhance its beauty (e.g. paint, varnish, lacquer). A further aspect to be considered under design is the scale of the furniture. Proportions should be pleasing in relation to other items of furniture and equipment located nearby and to the dimensions of the room or area itself.

2. **Comfort.** Trends and preferences of library users change regularly. Several years ago there was a movement away from the privacy of the study carrel to open furniture. Today in many academic libraries there is increasing demand once again for facilities for serious, uninterrupted study. In audiovisual centers, both types of seating should be provided. While the carrel remains most suitable for certain types of media use, more casual study

environments suit other media formats (for example group TV viewing). Comfort implies a state of ease free from any distress or pain. Furniture of correct size and proportion will be comfortable to use for a variety of activities such as working, viewing, reading, or relaxing. To obtain comfort, attention must be given to factors such as height and pitch of seat, area of work surface, and color and light-reflecting qualities of work surface.

3. **Ease of adjustment.** This is a consideration with shelving, for example, which may need adjustment with regard to height and width in order to accommodate a variety of material. Stackable chairs and tables may be considered to cater to a wide variety of group sizes. Adjustable screens are essential if various types of projection equipment are to be used.

4. **Repairs.** Furniture, fixtures, and equipment in the audiovisual center are likely to be subjected to heavy use if not abuse. Factors such as durability and ease of repair should be considered when purchases are made, surfaces must withstand scratching, joints should be strong, and the design should be sturdy.

5. **Safety.** Planners should consider safety factors with regard to furniture and equipment. Sharp edges on tables, exposed wiring in audiovisual carrels, chairs that may slip when tipped backward by the reader, unstable shelving units, and weak bolts and joints are areas of which to be aware.

6. **Service life.** This is not easy to assess at the time of purchase, as much will depend on the amount of use made of an item. Upholstered chairs wear easily, but most will last for at least seven years.

Work surfaces should be accessible to the user, and designed so that there is no wasted space. There should be sufficient space to accommodate a variety of material yet still permit the user ample space to work without feeling crowded.[18] Table surfaces should be light in color, as the contrast of white pages against dark surfaces may cause eye strain. The audiovisual carrel remains an important part of the seating allocation of the audiovisual center, and is also a storage unit for a wide variety of equipment. The individual carrel may be merely a semiprivate study cubicle, or it may be a sophisticated multimedia station incorporating sound and picture in a variety of configurations.[19] Large items of equipment will often be placed permanently in carrels because of weight and wear and tear suffered when transported frequently. When carrels house equipment, they should be oriented so that hardware is easily visible to staff as well as library patrons, in order to discourage vandalism. Smaller items of equipment, such as audiocassette players, will last longer and need repair less often if charged out from the lending desk rather than being built into tables or carrels. In most cases where media hardware is to be placed in open library spaces, carrels are the ideal location; they offer a measure of privacy, reduce noise, may be easily wired for electrical power, and they may be custom-built to accommodate certain types of equipment. An audiovisual carrel has the following approximate dimensions:[20]

Overall		
height:	1,200–1,525 mm	(47–60ins)
Tabletop		
height:	710–760 mm	(28–30ins)
Overall		
width:	1,220 mm	(48ins)
Overall		
depth:	1,070 mm	(42ins)
Worksurface		
depth:	840 mm	(33ins)

These dimensions vary according to individual requirements. Larger units may be required to accommodate two or three users at any one time. A sturdy design able to withstand some abuse should be used, and the working surface should be scratch resistant.

Storage and Security

Both conservation and security requirements should be considered when deciding how and where media will be housed.[21] Both media software and hardware are expensive to replace, and it is important that careful control is maintained to safeguard it. A strict circulation policy is recommended. On the other hand, however,

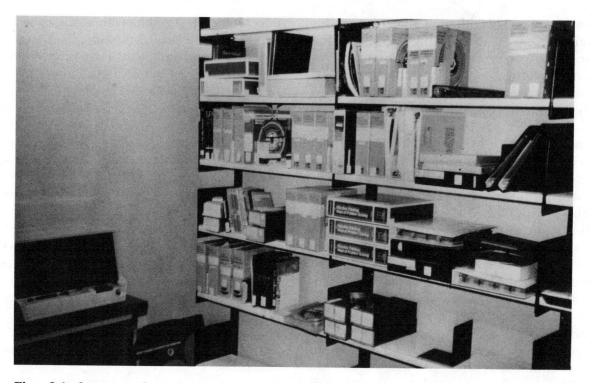

Fig. 9.1. Storage of Audiovisual Material (University of the Witwatersrand Library, Johannesburg)

the collection should be as accessible as possible (see Fig. 9.1). Too many locked cupboards and cabinets may cause unnecessary delay in service, inefficient use of staff time, and user frustration. The librarian needs to seek a compromise between control and accessibility suited to his particular situation.

Most types of media are best stored vertically (e.g. phonograph records, tapes, slides, photographs, videocassettes). A wide variety of storage cabinets and containers is available for different media, and the design of such equipment should afford a logical arrangement of material and easy access to it by the user. Where shelving is used, these should not be separated from the main audiovisual user areas by partitions; they should be easily accessible. Double-sided shelving in rows with stack centers at 1.37 m (4′ 6″), allowing a clear aisle width of at least 915 mm (3ft) is suitable. Island shelving should be avoided within user areas, except where counter-height units are used to define spaces. Hicks and Tillin[22] have outlined the various types of storage available:

- *Standard shelving:* For 8mm and 16mm films, audiovisual kits, any material in a container, audiorecordings.
- *Files:* Vertical files for unframed pictures, pamphlets, folded charts, transparencies. Horizontal files for larger posters, charts, and maps.
- *Cabinets (mobile and stationary):* For framed art prints, disc recordings, filmstrips (shallow compartmentalized drawers), multimedia (such as tapes, cartridges, slides, transparencies), microform, motion pictures (equipped with racks), records and tapes, photographic material.
- *Racks:* May be used to house prints, records, maps, and charts.
- *Modular shelving units:* For a wide variety of media housed in trays, boxes, or containers.
- *Special units:* For particular purposes such as browsing bins for records, see-through panels for slides.

Factors that should be considered regarding storage include the cost of specialized containers, identifying the items easily, damage through excessive handling, the ease with which the user can locate material (reduced if too many separate sequences are introduced), and special environmental conditions for certain types of audiovisual material.

Storage space is also required for audiovisual equipment. The area should be provided with 305 mm (12ins)- and 380 mm (15ins)- deep adjustable shelving. Aisles should be wide enough to facilitate easy movement of equipment, and sufficient space should be left free of stacks to allow for housing large items of equipment on trolleys.

Handling materials should be made as simple as possible. If trolleys are used to transport the larger items of audiovisual equipment (e.g. TV monitors, projectors), providing shelves, counters, and table surfaces at the same height as the trolleys will facilitate movement.

It is also advisable to provide an area for dealing with repairs, as audiovisual equipment has a propensity to break down, especially when used by a wide variety of people. It is unlikely that the average library will have its own repair/maintenance staff, but if space is provided in the form of a repair bench, with power outlets and suitable shelves, repairs by outside service technicians may often be effected on the premises, thereby saving time and costs. In addition to the work bench, the area should contain space for checking equipment, storing minor replacement parts, and inspecting films and tapes for possible damage.[23] An area of 20m² (±215ft²) is suggested.

Traffic and Supervision

Space allocated to administrative areas will depend on local circumstances. Audiovisual materials will be borrowed, equipment serviced and loaned, items ordered and processed, and a variety of records kept. It is likely that a circulation counter will be necessary, as well as more private office space for professional staff.

Although the audiovisual center should be designed and located so as to be highly visible and easily accessible to all students entering the li-

brary, heavy traffic routes penetrating or separating major elements of the center must be avoided. Design should provide supervisory personnel at their work stations with good visual control over the public areas of the center, including entrances and exits, reading room and shelving areas. The audiovisual center should also be accessible from the exterior of the building via ramps, to facilitate transport by trolley of equipment on loan or being sent for repair.

Physical Requirements of the Various Media

1. **Listening equipment for audio recordings.** The trend is away from the old dial access systems toward providing individually controlled players with headphones. The players may be grouped in one part of the center to facilitate supervision and servicing. In addition it will also be necessary to make provision for group listening. A small study room will serve well as long as it can accommodate a table and a few chairs and has a source of electrical power. Larger groups may be accommodated in larger study or seminar rooms. Headphones produce enough fidelity for most general listening, but not for advanced music study. For this purpose some librarians will wish to have one or more rooms equipped with built-in speakers, which should be located at ear level. Unless these listening rooms can be fully isolated, they should be given careful acoustic treatment.

2. **Television/video tape players.** Some new video tape recorders require only electrical power outlets, thus eliminating the need for coaxial cables. However, if a university has a campus-wide closed-circuit system, provision should be made for using closed-circuit television within the building.[24] Even though many campuses have not yet made use of television in their teaching programs, it is certain that where they do, the library is the easiest and most accessible place for the student to go to view a program. This type of media is usually housed permanently in carrels, located within easy reach of a service desk, with

cassettes or videodiscs stored on shelves or in cabinets nearby.

3. **Cassette-tape recorders.** Small cassette-tape broadcasting systems with a loop antenna are convenient where a group of students, with their own headphones, wishes to listen to a tape at the same time. This facility is popular, especially where comfortable furniture is provided. It is likely that the library will require many cassette players, and because of the problem of theft, they should be stored either behind the service desk or in locked cupboards, and issued against a user's identity card or deposit. There is no specialized furniture for housing these items; in most cases they are stored on shelves.

4. **Computer instructional keyboards and microcomputers.** These are now frequently provided for students, and it is only a matter of time before most libraries will need to make them available (see Fig. 9.2). Most libraries have installed patron computers in the general audiovisual area of the library, where the noise created by keyboards, disc

drives, and printers blends with the noise level already existing in such areas, and this can work well. However, in quieter environments alternative arrangements may have to be made, and Thompson[25] has described how the Wilmette Public Library (Illinois) solved the problem. A considered decision was taken as to the location of the patron computer room, and an area 12′ 6″ × 8′ 6″ (3.8 m × 2.6 m) was partitioned off. These partitions were constructed of plasterboard (the lower ⅓) and double glazing (the top ⅔) to provide a more congenial space for users with sufficient soundproofing. A 12 ft counter (3.7 m), 26.5 ins high (0.7 m) and 30 ins (0.8 m) deep was built along the partition, placed so that users face outward into the body of the library while the computer screen remains private as far as other library users are concerned. The counter accommodates three work stations, and there is space along the back wall for shelving. Although this type of arrangement is suitable for the majority of "public" computer facilities, computer tech-

Fig. 9.2. Computer-Assisted Learning (Brigham Young University Library, Provo, Utah, U.S.A.)

nology is evolving so rapidly that planners should seek specialized advice at an early stage in planning this part of the audiovisual center.

5. **Slides and slide/tape programs.** These are most easily used in individual carrels where the equipment may be semipermanently stored.

6. **Films, overhead transparencies.** Facilities for projection require careful consideration. Good-quality image is required on the screen if students are to watch in comfort with minimal visual and postural stress. Screen size should be scaled to room size (see Fig. 9.3). This is determined by taking the length of the

room and dividing by six for optimum viewing and by eight for marginal viewing. The front seats should be at a distance of twice the screen width (2W) away from the screen, while the back seats should be 6W away. The ideal viewing angle is 30° on either side of the center, but is acceptable up to 45°. The best viewing area is in the center, and thus side aisles should be used in preference to a center aisle. The screen should be mounted 1.2 m (4ft) off the floor, so that people may see over the heads of others.[26] Corner screens are possible, but not as ideal as front screens, as they lead to postural tension in the viewer. If a corner screen is used in a room with windows on one wall, it

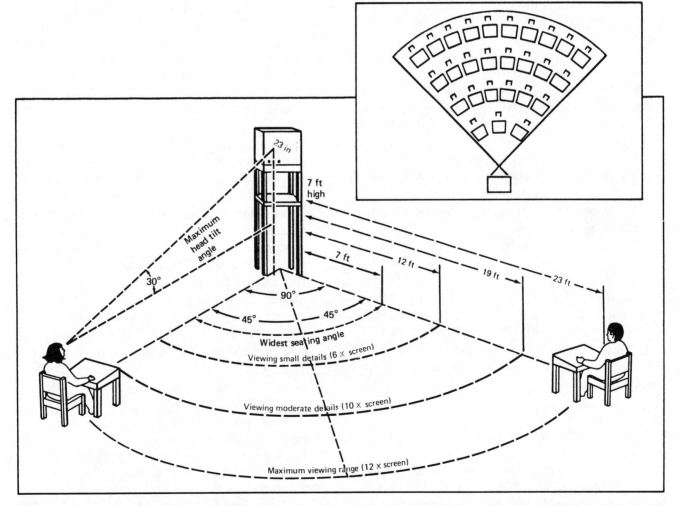

Fig. 9.3. Screen Size in Relation to Room Size. *Source:* Robert Heinrich, James D. Russell, and Michael Molenda. *Instructional Media and the New Technologies of Instruction.* New York: Macmillan, 1985. Reprinted with permission of Macmillan Publishing Company from *Instructional Media and the New Technologies of Instruction* by Robert Heinrich, James D. Russell, and Michael Molenda. Copyright © Macmillan 1985.

should be placed in the corner closest to the windows so that it faces away from direct light.

7. **Television.** The general rule for group viewing of television is one person per 25 mm (1in) of the screen display diagonal. No viewer should be closer than 2.14 m (7ft), especially in the case of color television. A viewing angle of 45° either side of center is marginally acceptable.

The following viewer distances are recommended for various types of audiovisual material:[27]

- *1W:* Recommended minimum distance for multiscreen viewing.
- *2W:* Distance at which 70% of total acuity takes place. Recommended minimum distance for most media.
- *3W:* Recommended maximum viewing distance for multiscreen viewing.
- *4W:* 80% total acuity. Recommended minimum distance for television viewing, and maximum for displays having exceptionally small symbols.
- *6W:* Recommended maximum for viewing most media, particularly commercially produced motion pictures.
- *10W:* Recommended ideal maximum distance for viewing television.
- *14W:* Traditional maximum distance for viewing television.

Useful detail regarding criteria for effective reproduction of various kinds of media, and the design factors that should be taken into consideration, may be found in *Instructional Media and the New Technologies of Instruction, 2nd ed. (New York: Wiley, 1985).*

Media Production Center

According to Lushington,[28] no media center may justifiably call itself such unless it has production facilities. Many audiovisual centers in academic libraries today are providing production space for use by academic staff and students. This may range from a well-equipped, acous-

tically treated complex consisting of a darkroom, model-making room, tape recording studio, and an area for charts and reprographics, to a general workroom of modest size containing a work counter, running water, and cupboard and shelving space. In either case, the underlying philosophy is that such facilities will act as a catalyst for innovative and effective teaching. Functions of the production area could include preparing and producing overhead transparencies, slides, slide/tape programs, visuals for videos, models, individualized instruction packages, audio materials, charts and graphs, brochures, pamphlets, and posters. Areas required for each function will vary with the size of the audiovisual center and of the university itself.

A useful guideline for space requirements in a media center is provided by the Indiana Department of Public Instruction.[29] Although devised primarily for school media programs, it has much relevance to university library audiovisual centers, and the main recommendations are summarized below:

1. Display and circulation of materials and equipment. Requires circulation desk, catalogues, display area. Space recommended: 500–800 ft^2 (47–75 m^2).
2. Individual reading, listening, viewing, study. Requires suitable tables and chairs, adequate power supply, audiovisual carrels. Space recommended: 12–15% of student body, at 30 ft^2 (28 m^2) per student.
3. Small group viewing and/or listening activities. Requires areas approximately 100 ft^2 (9 m^2) each, acoustically treated, provided with screen. Space recommended: 200 ft^2 (20 m^2).
4. Large viewing area. Equivalent of a classroom area, fully equipped.
5. Administrative activities. 150 ft^2 (15 m^2) per professional staff member.
6. Production and processing of materials. Requires area with sink, power points, counter work surface and storage. Space recommended: 300–500 ft^2 (30–47 m^2). A darkroom of 150 ft^2 (15 m^2) may be provided.
7. Storage of equipment, materials, and supplies. Requires storage area with controlled

temperature and humidity and stack area for audiovisual material. Space recommended for audiovisual material: 400 ft² (40 m²). Space for storage of equipment: 1,200 ft² (110 m²).

8. Video and audio tape recording. Requires a soundproof area. Space recommendation: 150 ft² (15 m²).

COMMENTS

One can see from the above that the effect of audiovisual development on the library is generally more pervasive than at first expected. There is little doubt that the impetus toward use of audiovisual material and the expansion of facilities in this field has come from the teaching side. This is possibly due to the realization that the lecture, followed perhaps by a question and answer session, is not necessarily the best method of conveying information. This is particularly applicable where there are increasing student numbers, and many who for reasons of their home background or inadequate schooling might have difficulty in coping with their courses. The library must take up the challenge of assisting actively in this educational role, and of utilizing the variety of information technologies available today.

REFERENCES

1. D.D. Hickey, "The impact of instructional technology on the future of academic librarianship," in *Academic Libraries by the Year 2000: Essays Honouring Jerrold Orne,* ed. H. Poole (New York: Bowker, 1977), p.40.
2. P.G. Ahlsted and P. Graham, "Media collections and services in academic libraries," *Library Trends,* Summer 1985, p.4.
3. M. Aston, "Information technology: here and now benefits," *ASLIB Proceedings,* vol.35, no.1, 1983, p.52.
4. S.N. Bunson, "Put a micro in the media center," *Instructional Innovator,* January 1984, p.29.
5. T.B. Wall, "Nonprint materials," *Library Trends,* Summer 1985, p.131.

6. R. Fothergill and I. Butchart. *Non-Book Materials in Libraries,* 2nd ed. (London: Bingley, 1984), p.259.
7. Wall, p.133.
8. Ibid.
9. W.S. Pierce, *Furnishing the Library Interior* (New York: Marcel Dekker, 1980), p.172.
10. Fothergill, p.260.
11. J. Moldstad, *Designing Facilities for Optimum Use of Instructional Technologies.* Workshop given at Instructa 1984, Rand Afrikaans University, Johannesburg, July 1984.
12. Fothergill, p.261.
13. Moldstad.
14. *Encyclopaedia of Educational Media Communications and Technology,* ed. D. Unwin and R. McAlcese (Westport, Conn.: Greenwood Press, 1978), p.485.
15. R. Sommer, quoted in *Encyclopaedia of Educational Media Communications and Technology* (Westport, Conn.: Greenwood Press, 1978), p.467.
16. J. Bock and L.R. La Jeunesse, "The Learning Resources Centre," *Library Journal Special Report No.3,* 1978, pp.26–29.
17. M. van Buren, "Design of library furniture," in *Reader on the Library Building,* ed. H.B. Schell (Englewood, Colo.: Microcard Editions Books, 1975), pp.301–4.
18. J. Sullivan, "Nine design factors for better learning," *Instructional Innovator,* March 1981, p.14.
19. Bock, p.32.
20. R.W. Spangenberg, "Human factors in the design of carrels for learning," *Audiovisual Communications Review,* vol.23, no.3, 1975, pp.325–26.
21. Wall, p.135.
22. W.B. Hicks and A.M. Tillin, *Developing Multi-Media Libraries* (New York: Bowker, 1970), p.92.
23. J.H. Moriarty, "New media facilities," in *Reader on the Library Building,* p.252.
24. R.E. Ellsworth, *Planning Manual for Academic Library Buildings* (Metuchen, N.J.: Scarecrow Press, 1973), p.91.
25. R.E. Thompson, "A Room of their own: optimal setting for patrons and patron computers," *Technical Services Quarterly,* vol.2, no.3/4, 1985, pp.73–91.
26. Moldstad.
27. Ibid.
28. N. Lushington and W.N. Mills, *Libraries Designed for Users: A Planning Handbook* (Hamden, Conn.: Library Professional Publications, 1980), p.183.
29. Indiana Department of Public Instruction, *Guidelines for Indiana School Media Programs,* 1978.

10 Space Management

The pressures of increasing student numbers and expanding research activities have led to an increase in the demand for space at the same time as financial restraints have placed firmer controls on the supply of space. These developments over the past few years have forced many universities in countries such as the United States and Great Britain for the first time in their histories to inquire seriously into the utilization of space. The relatively new discipline that integrates the space requirements of the physical facility with the planning process of the library as a growing, changing organization is known as space management.[1] Academic libraries today are constantly undergoing change and rearrangement, and good space management will be needed if they are to remain flexible, efficient, and comfortable.

MODULAR PLANNING

In considering space, it is necessary to determine how usable that space is. The space becomes functional when it can *actually* be used. Assignable areas are those that can *potentially* be used. Cohen[2] gives an example of a space 300 m long by 3 m wide. The assignable area is 900 m² but in fact the usability of the space is greatly impaired by its long, narrow shape, and it could probably be used only for wall-mounted shelving, the majority of space being used for corridor access. The total assignable space may appear generous, but usability is questionable. Usability increases in open plan square or rectangular areas, with columns placed at regular intervals. This is known as modular construction, a method that

has been used extensively in libraries for several decades.

First described and advocated in the United States in the 1930s by Angus Snead Macdonald, architect and library shelving manufacturer, the modular library was strongly supported in those early years by Ellsworth, librarian at the University of Iowa at the time. The concept did away with permanent load-bearing internal walls, and replaced them with carefully distributed columns that would bear the weight of the upper levels. Air conditioning and electrical ducts were contained in false ceilings, and flush lighting fixtures became possible for the first time. By the 1960s this type of library construction had been developed to its most ideal form, and new library buildings around the world were built according to these principles.

The modular library made possible an easy integration of reading and stack spaces; the elimination of thick walls and elaborate decoration proved economical; electrical outlets and ventilation ducts were easy to install and change; and most importantly, flexible use of space became possible.[3] Modular planning thus ensures that any part of the building may be used for any purpose within reason, with the obvious exception of the core areas containing stairways, toilets, elevators, and mechanical facilities. This flexibility is necessary if library buildings are to adapt to changing needs.

Modular planning does have its weaknesses. First, it tends to cost more. The further apart the columns are, the stronger the floors have to be. As column spacing increases, structural precautions such as tensioning of reinforced steel and use of higher-strength concrete become necessary. The depth of the structural floor system increases, and extra height is added to the building. Second, no one column spacing is ideal for all library purposes, although many librarians agree on either 22' 6" or 27 ft (6.86 m or 8.24 m).[4] Third, some librarians on moving into a modular building have assumed that because it could adapt easily, it was unnecessary to plan in advance, and have found themselves within a year wanting to make changes. These changes may be easy and relatively inexpensive, but if they involve lighting, ventilation, and internal partitioning, they can be costly. However, despite these drawbacks, there is wide agreement that modular planning and regular column spacing are desirable because they provide the necessary flexibility and freedom in planning for the future. As Thompson[5] points out, although the librarian is not concerned with most aspects of modular construction such as material, strength, and shape, leaving these matters to the architect and engineer, he is directly interested in the positioning of the columns. If they are placed at intervals inappropriate for the library's economic operation, results will be disastrous.

The distance between the center of one column and that of the next depends on the answers to a number of questions outlined by Metcalf:[6]

1. **What is the size of column necessary to hold up the building without bearing walls?** This will depend on the method of construction—whether the columns are primarily steel, or whether they are concrete reinforced with steel. Another factor is the height of the building. In a multistory building, the columns will have to be larger or closer together in order to support the building. The width of a column at right angles to the direction of the bookstacks should be no greater than the depth of the double-faced stack. If this is 450 mm (18 ins) from front to back, the column should not exceed this size. However, it may be necessary to make it wider in the other direction to provide sufficient support.

2. **How will the ventilating, heating, mechanical, and wiring systems be arranged?** If the service ducts are carried up through the center of the columns or through outside walls, they create a certain amount of fixed function. It is becoming more usual to run them along the ceiling at regular intervals, either concealed within a false ceiling or in ducts projecting below it.

3. **What is the acceptable length of shelves or stack units?** In Britain and the United States (as well as many other countries), 915 mm (3ft) is the standard length of library shelving. The standard distance between centers of stack ranges is generally 1.37 m (4' 6"). Twice this is 2.74 m (9ft), and with a standard shelf length of 915 mm (3ft), interchangeability of direction is possible.

4. **Length of stack range** before reaching a cross aisle is important. The only justification for long ranges is to save the space taken up by the cross aisle. The length of the ranges should bear some relation to their use and the width of the aisle, e.g. a very long range would be unsuitable for heavy open access use and narrow aisle width, but would be acceptable in a storage area.

5. **Should the columns be spaced equidistantly in both directions?** An advantage of the square bay is that it makes it possible under certain conditions to shift bookstacks (or any other equipment) through 90°. However, care should be taken regarding lighting.

In any library a 6.1 m (20ft) distance between columns is the minimum suggested. Anything less will severely affect utilization of space, and it will be difficult to design the interior properly. The column spacing generally recommended in academic libraries is 6.86 m (22' 6"), 7.79 m (25' 6"), or 8.24 m (27ft). If bookstacks fall between columns, they require a clear space that is a multiple of 915 mm (3ft), plus a little space for stack ends.

Ellsworth, in his book *Planning Manual for Academic Library Buildings (1973)*,[7] gives a clear description of modular dimensions. The size of the module depends primarily on cost versus book storage efficiency. The longer the distance between columns, the higher the cost. However, if the distance is too short, a multitude of columns will get in the way of readers and bookstacks.

The most the librarian can do is define the problem and talk to the architect about the various options and their advantages and disadvantages; the architect and his engineer must make the final decision.

FLOOR SIZE

There has been some discussion as to the optimal size of the floors making up a library (Cohen and Lushington), and it is generally recommended that they do not exceed 1,860–2,790 m² on one level (20,000–30,000 ft²). A number of libraries contain areas of up to 4,650 m² (50,000 ft²) per level, but very large spaces become difficult to control, more service points are usually required, and hence more staff needed.[8] It is generally advisable to reduce horizontal distances and the use of ground areas and provide more levels when this stage is reached. Careful thought should be given to optimum size, not only from the point of view of use, but also cost. The greater the number of levels, the lower the roof cost; the fewer the number of levels, the lower the wall cost. Floor areas should be planned for flexibility so that they may be easily subdivided if necessary, care being taken of exit and entry points, the stairwell, and the plumbing, electrical, and mechanical core. Cohen[9] suggests that in any library the length of the space should reflect the width, and this ratio should not exceed 2:1, otherwise a long, narrow, and somewhat impractical space will result. The nearer to square the building is, the more economies will be achieved in terms of cost and efficiency of use.

BUILDING HEIGHT

It is also suggested that ideally buildings contain no more than three floors. The best possible situation would be a building stepped down on a hillside with the main entrance on the second level, such as University of Denver Library. Users would then be required to walk one flight of stairs either up or down to reach any part of the library, and this is the most functional and

economic design in terms of traffic patterns. Obviously every situation is different, and much depends on the total size of the library as well as the site. Metcalf[10] outlines four factors that determine the height of a building in relation to function:

a) Generally, the larger each level, the lower the percentage of total space required for core areas and the smaller the proportion of outside wall to total floor area.
b) When library patrons use primarily those sections of the library which are no more than two levels above or below the entrance level, lifts need be installed only for the use of handicapped persons and staff with book trolleys and equipment. This results in substantial savings on transportation. A library situated on sloping ground as described above provides this feature.
c) If library staff are to provide service on each level, fewer levels will require less staff, an important factor when long hours of opening are envisaged.
d) The entrance or main level of any library should contain as many of the central services as possible, in order to control traffic, keep large numbers of people from passing through quiet study areas, and maximize efficiency of use.

Thus the number of levels in a library is important from a cost and functional point of view. Aesthetics should also be considered.

Having looked at the physical structure of the library with regard to space management, library planners must then give careful consideration to the internal environment and the way in which this will affect the users of the library in terms of their needs and comfort.

LIBRARY ENVIRONMENT

Although much emphasis today is placed on the library's ability to satisfy users' needs through the availability of a variety of materials and services, it is also very desirable that the environment contribute to their library experience in a positive way. Patrons who can relate to and enjoy the atmosphere of the library are more likely to return than those who merely obtain the item of information they require. Mason[11] states:

The interior design is the most important single element in generating the use of any library dedicated to serving undergraduates. . . . If a library feels good to be in, it will be used even though the air conditioning freezes, the lighting obscures, the bookstock dwindles and the staff offends. Though the architect lead the student through labyrinthine ways, yet will he follow if it feels good to be there.

Unfortunately the library's internal physical appearance is sometimes neglected, and bad design of the building and its facilities can become a barrier to library use. Too often the planning team does not visualize correctly the various functions of the library and their interrelationship. Too seldom do librarians bother to find out what their users really need in a library environment. Methods of teaching today encourage students to take more initiative in the learning process, and thus they make greater demands on the library and its services than in the past. If the librarian is to provide a good service and manage his space effectively, his physical plant must assist in this learning process. What is the impact of environment on behavior, productivity, and on job satisfaction? What is the effect of the workplace on human performance?[12] These questions relate to both users of the library building and the staff who work therein.

The increasing use of new communication and computing technologies as well as a wide range of audiovisual materials have given rise to new functions and uses of libraries, and these are reflected in a need for new design characteristics. Lushington[13] suggests that the following elements should be taken into consideration:

- integrated design to accommodate a wide range of media;
- centralized information and service center run by professional staff from which various services may radiate;
- flexibility of facilities and equipment to make change easy and possible;
- spaces of various shapes and sizes to ensure user choices;
- appropriate storage for materials of various types, arranged for rapid and convenient retrieval;
- easy accessibility of users to services and library materials;

- properly designed graphics, furniture, lighting and functional relationships which contribute greatly towards the creation of an attractive and comfortable environment.

It is not always easy to achieve all these design objectives. For example, if one is designing areas for specific functions, it is difficult to include the necessary design detail yet maintain flexibility. Central services need to be provided, yet private spaces for individuals must also exist. A staff presence on each level of the library introduces an element of control, yet the user must not feel that his freedom and privacy are being reduced. The resolution of these conflicting concepts is the key to good design.

Lushington[14] summarizes clearly the need for more awareness on the part of library planners of users and their environmental requirements. While recognizing that most libraries are flexible in that they feature open plan modular buildings with movable partitions, numerous electrical outlet points, and excellent lighting and air conditioning facilities throughout, he emphasizes that library planners faced with a large flexible space must be careful not to create a lifeless desert that does not cater to the varied requirements of different library service areas. "A flexible space can be the beginning of a useful design, but it must be followed with careful selection of furnishings, equipment, lighting and graphics to breathe color and life into the library activities that will take place there."[11]

The interior design should simplify the library experience of the users. They should be able to find what they want easily and without walking long distances, and they should be provided with choices in terms of environment. Library spaces may be either active or passive. The former will provide gregarious users, or those who do not have much time to spare, with seating and facilities in noisy, busy areas such as those containing current journals, new books, newspapers, and audiovisual materials. Group seating as well as informal chairs are frequently found in these sections, and the atmosphere may be further emphasized by use of bright colors, graphics, and the proximity of reference and information services. Active areas are generally located near the entrance of the library where traffic is heaviest. Passive areas are popular with those users who wish to study for longer periods, and they include individual or group seating located well away from the entrance area. These areas provide an environment where there is little distraction both visually and audibly, and where care has been taken to reduce noise levels through the use of acoustic material on floors and ceilings and the appropriate location of bookstacks.

Most libraries provide a wide range of seating choices. A possible combination suggested by Lushington[15] is as follows:

Lounge seating:	5%
Individual rooms:	Up to 5%
Individual desks/carrels:	Up to 70%
Group rooms (5–10 persons):	Up to 5%
Group seating at tables (4 persons):	15%

Metcalf[16] suggests slightly different allocations:

Lounge seating:	not more than 15%
Individual desks/carrels:	up to 85%
Group seating (4 persons):	not more than 20%

Group study rooms are an important development in the provision of informal seating in academic libraries. Students studying the same subject may wish to meet to discuss problems or assignments, and a study room in the library where they will not disturb others is the ideal place. Such areas may also be used by faculty for seminars or tutorial classes. In most libraries where such facilities have been provided, they have been well utilized. Whether these rooms are designated "smoking rooms" depends on the policy of the particular institution and/or library.

Generally, however, library planning today places emphasis on individual readers and their environment. Most readers use the library to obtain information and study, requiring a certain level of visual and aural privacy. With the development of a wide variety of study carrels that take up approximately the same amount of space as tables, it is now possible to give readers both a choice of seating and the privacy they

need. It is important to avoid an impression of overcrowding and congestion, as this more than anything will affect negatively the attitude of the user to the library. Tables with chairs on both sides should be at least 1.2 m (4 ft) across to give readers sufficient space. It should be borne in mind that so-called 4-, 6-, and 8-seat tables rarely accommodate the stated number of readers and are thus uneconomical in terms of space usage. Despite having the requisite work surface area, visual disturbance is generally too great, and readers will seek a more private location.

The library planner should try to provide as much variety of seating and environment as possible, keeping the user's comfort in mind at all times. For example, it is not sufficient merely to provide study carrels for the serious student. It should be remembered that most people, when they concentrate, prefer to protect their backs and sides—they are not comfortable in situations where they may be approached from behind. Thus carrels should not face away from passages and traffic lanes, but should rather be parallel to them. People working in noisy, active areas seem to be more tolerant, and generally do not mind which way they face. Personal observations of student behavior indicate that:

- The group study room is helpful as students sometimes like to work together in small groups.
- Small lounges where casual seating is provided are popular, as are smoking rooms.
- Carrels are greatly appreciated, especially near examination time.
- The rooms that work well are not tidy and neat; they are well-used and look it.
- A cluster of different reading facilities allows some users to look out of a window; others to sit in lounge chairs and put their feet up; others to study in work carrels adjacent to the bookstacks.

Another factor that may affect the user is ceiling height. High ceilings seem to encourage movement, while low ceilings have the opposite effect. For this reason soaring ceilings, if they exist at all, should be confined to the foyer or main service area. If found in reading rooms, they will have a negative effect, as users, once seated, may feel small and insignificant. This could partly explain why study carrels are invariably so popular. The protection afforded by the carrel sides makes the immediate surroundings more human.[17]

Planners need to be aware of changes in the sociological habits of readers and they must recognize new demands. They must study and assess the needs, preferences, and peculiarities of their particular user population, and provide imaginative yet functional furniture. High-quality furniture along with the architectural quality of the building will go a long way toward providing an attractive physical environment. An economic and spacious library that supplies an efficient service is a positive asset. An even more positive asset is a facility that is functional and aesthetically pleasing at the same time. Good-looking space can do a great deal for a library's image.

As far as library staff space is concerned, opinions vary. The conclusions of several surveys indicate that although working conditions are important, recognition of achievement, responsibility, and motivation are even more so. Although environment does make a difference to productivity and job satisfaction, there is no simple relationship between the environment and complex human behavior. Realistically, office design will not cause people to behave in a certain way, but it can act as a "support system" for staff.[18] A well-designed office provides an atmosphere where people can think, act, feel, and work productively and comfortably for long stretches of time.

The Buffalo Organization for Social and Technological Innovation[19] undertook a study of environmental effects on work spaces in the late 1970s, and because a large percentage of those surveyed worked in the public sector, the results are of interest to library managers. Factors directly affecting job satisfaction were floor area, temperature/air quality, lighting, noise, ease of communication, comfort, participation in the planning and designing of own work spaces, and privacy. The totally open plan office was found, surprisingly, to be least satisfactory for communication. The open plan office with partitioning on three sides of each work station was found to facilitate far better communication, as well as providing much needed privacy. The need for off-duty space for personnel dealing with the public for long periods of time was clearly highlighted.

When considering space management in staff areas today, careful consideration of the effects of computer equipment on staff work stations is necessary (see chapter 8). The introduction of the new technology can result in ergonomic problems, possible health risks associated with long-term exposure to terminal screens, and problems with the very repetitive work involved in some automated procedures.[20] Careful selection of furniture and equipment is necessary. Desks to house terminals or microcomputers should be slightly lower (50 mm or 2 ins) than normal desk height, and should be fitted with wiring channels underneath and outlet plugs on top. The chairs at these work stations should be much more sophisticated than regular office chairs, with adjustable height, seat tilt, and backrest position. Long hours in front of a terminal may cause severe discomfort if attention is not given to these aspects. Each individual work station must be located in the correct relationship to others, to ensure a simple and effective work flow. This alters radically when systems are changed from manual to automated, and discussion with the staff of relevant departments is recommended. It must be borne in mind at all times that more space will be needed for each member of staff using a terminal, microcomputer or wordprocessor than was necessary for manual operations in the past.

In summary, with libraries adapting to change and the new technology, library planners should be aware of the size and type of spaces required, as well as the furniture and equipment they contain or are likely to contain. They should also be aware to a certain degree of the psychology of human nature. If they take into consideration both the information and environmental needs of patrons and staff, the facility is likely to be popular and well used. Good space management will ensure comfort, productivity, and efficient and happy use of the facilities provided.

REFERENCES

1. E. Cohen and A. Cohen, *Automation, Space Management and Productivity* (New York: Bowker, 1981, p.73).
2. Ibid., p.76.
3. A. Toffler, "Libraries," in *Reader on the Library Building,* ed. H.B. Schell (Englewood, Colo.: Microcard Editions Books, 1975), p.33.
4. G. Thompson, *Planning and Design of Library Buildings,* 2nd ed. (London: Architectural Press, 1977), p.72.
5. Ibid., p.72.
6. K.D. Metcalf, "Modular planning and physical dimensions," *in* H. Faulkner-Brown (ed.), *Planning the Academic Library* (Newcastle-upon-Tyne: Oriel Press, 1971), pp.35–37.
7. R.E. Ellsworth, *Planning Manual for Academic Library Buildings* (Metuchen, N.J.: Scarecrow Press, 1973), p.115.
8. Cohen, p.119.
9. Ibid., p.117.
10. K.D. Metcalf, *Planning Academic and Research Library Buildings* (New York: McGraw-Hill, 1965), p.74.
11. E. Mason, *Mason on Library Buildings* (Metuchen, N.J.: Scarecrow Press, 1980), p.49.
12. J.M. Isacco, "Work spaces, satisfaction and productivity in libraries," *Library Journal,* May 1, 1985, p.27.
13. N. Lushington and W.N. Mills, *Libraries Designed for Users: A Planning Handbook* (Hamden, Conn.: Library Professional Publications, 1980), p.16.
14. Ibid., p.17.
15. Ibid., p.139.
16. Metcalf, *Planning Academic and Research Library Buildings,* p.390.
17. Cohen, p.109.
18. Isacco, p.28.
19. Buffalo Organization for Social and Technological Innovation, "The Impact of Office Environment on Productivity and Quality of Working Life," [preliminary findings], n.d., quoted by Isacco.
20. D. Waters, "New technology in the task environment of Australian university libraries," *Australian Library Journal,* February, 1986, p.13.

11 Conclusion

> Form follows function, and function follows time. Libraries are planned to reflect what users do—or what librarians want them to do. But users change; and then librarians; and finally, the libraries.[1]

If attitudes, systems, or environments are subjected to questioning and are found to be inadequate, change occurs. The libraries that are built today are a response to the turbulent developments of recent years. They have changed to meet the information needs of more demanding users, to use the technology available, and to survive as viable entities in the information market. Librarians recognize that libraries may have to compete against a proliferation of commercial information storage and retrieval vendors in the years ahead, and that adaptation to change is essential.

Academic library architecture has evolved from the monumental excesses of the nineteenth century through the simple, functional designs of the 1960s and 1970s to the somewhat more complex styles of the 1980s. If the recent buildings constructed do not seem to be entirely satisfactory, this is possibly because libraries function better in the simple buildings of the 1960s.[2] When librarians are faced with problems of space shortage, limited budgets, increasingly varied demands from users, and outmoded manual systems that are unable to cope with workloads, their best solution is to build a flexible, functional library able to accommodate the wide variety of materials and equipment necessary today. As Rohlf[3] emphasizes they will *not* be assisted in their activities by enclosed courtyards, skylights, and atriums that force people to walk around large areas, nor by architectural lighting that fails to illuminate adequately the lower shelves of the bookstacks. Awkward shapes and complex traffic patterns, large glass areas that increase heat and glare and force air conditioning machinery to work harder, and indulgences on the part of the architect such as a high ceiling in the main hall and grand entrances, may add aesthetically to a building, but always at the expense of function.

The importance of function is seen particularly in the design and layout of the main floor of an academic library. It is essential that the architect be aware of what users require of a library, how they use the services provided, how they relate to the library staff, and how the latter relate to each other. Ease of use and efficiency are essential.

The entrance area should be attractive and welcoming, with circulation and information services immediately available and major routes clearly defined. Simplicity, color, and good-quality finishes are important. A circulation desk that includes short-loan and interlibrary loan functions in one central location serves to contain much of the traffic close to the entrance, reduces disturbance in other areas, and does not waste the time of users who merely wish to return or collect a book. Where the short-loan collection cannot be housed at the circulation desk (usually when it is too large), it should be located within close proximity on the main floor.

If there is sufficient space to locate technical processing departments on the main floor, this provides accessibility of information for both staff members and users and easy contact between the two when necessary. The spatial relationships of these departments must be carefully conceived. The point of delivery of library material should be located alongside or directly under the book and serial acquisitions departments, and these in turn should be adjacent to the cataloguing department. The passage of material to the shelves may be further facilitated by placing cataloguing in proximity to the circulation department, so that new (or recatalogued) items may pass directly to the sorting section and thence to display shelves or bookstacks. Locating technical processing departments on the main level places these staff within easy reach of the catalogues, the major reference collection, and bibliographic sources.

Bookstacks and study areas should be located on levels other than the main level. This provides the serious student with quiet surroundings and a study station in close proximity to the subject material in which he is interested. This is the way in which most academic libraries are designed today. Students and other users of academic libraries vary in their seating preferences, and a wide variety of study stations should be provided, ranging from group study lounges to private carrels.

Locating the main floor at ground level with floors above and below appears to be the most efficient design. Traffic within the library and distances to be traversed are reduced to a minimum. This is evidenced at the universities of Denver and of Northern Iowa libraries, which both function extremely well.

The needs of the user should be considered by the library planner. Drinking water fountains, clocks, public telephones for both external and campus use, coat hooks in study areas, typewriters, "public" computers, and equipment such as calculators, staplers, punches, and guillotines—all tend to make the user's library experience more pleasant. A "communications room" on each level of the library (e.g. at Stanford's Cecil H. Green Library), which contains a microfiche or online access point to the catalogues, telephone, directories, dictionaries, library guides, plans of library layout, and photocopiers is a highly recommended feature. Such facilities are greatly appreciated by users.

An area in which American libraries often surpass those in other parts of the world is that of interior decoration. Despite financial limitations, the use of an interior design consultant is fre-

quently part of the planning and building process, and the results are extremely positive. Expert advice on the use of color, texture, type of surface, furniture design, graphics, signage, and creation of atmosphere, as well as attention given to details such as door handles and light switches, all contribute to a pleasing coordination of elements. No matter how beautiful the building may be architecturally, its real beauty lies in its interior, and success in this area encourages better use of library facilities, makes it more efficient and easier to work in, and more attractive to users and staff. A good example of interior decoration is the Penrose Library at the University of Denver, where good use of color and graphics has transformed internal spaces. Wall graphics not only create cheerful study areas but assist in the location of subject fields by color coding. Staff offices have been changed from small, windowless spaces into bright, attractive work environments through the use of colored and reflective mirror tiles arranged in abstract designs on internal walls. Signs with letters 500 mm (20 ins) tall direct users to information and service points.

Once the various functions of a university library and their spatial interrelationships have been carefully considered, the question as to how much space to allocate to each arises. Although not prescriptive, space standards do provide a guideline for library planners. Consideration must be taken of both the positive and negative aspects of standards, and librarians should be knowledgeable of the situation in their own particular country and how this relates to an ideal situation. In South African universities, for example, space and cost norms are expected to have a negative effect on physical development, especially in those older universities where sizable collections already exist, or where decentralized systems, which are wasteful of space, have developed. In relating size to numbers of students, the government has effectively put an end to the natural growth of academic libraries. In the United Kingdom, many established universities have to cope with overcrowded shelves and relegation of lesser-used material to storage, again because of governmental restrictions on the size of university libraries. In the United

States, library space standards tend to differ from state to state, but are generally used as guidelines, especially where financial limitations are placed on the construction of a new building, or where standardized information is required for comparative purposes. The procedures are neither rigid nor compulsory.

Many involved in the educational process have expressed concern regarding limitations on size. The university library is not a static tool but a dynamic part of the teaching process. It cannot be of constant size if it is to build up research collections.[4] Ellsworth[5] is of the opinion that space formulae usually become a barrier to good planning for an institution that wishes to experiment with new instructional concepts and innovative library programs. However, the bibliographic, economic, and enrollment situation today is such that most libraries will have to make fundamental changes in the way they operate. The solution to growth in these areas, Orne[6] suggests, is not more books, more buildings, and more librarians. It is new service patterns, new concepts of collection management, and coordinated utilization of technological resources.

Once spaces required in a new library have been established, the library planner must then consider the nature of these spaces, their structural and physical requirements and the way in which they will best serve their purpose, both now and in the future. Flexibility is always the keyword, as change is inevitable. It is certain that the next decade will see automation spread to every aspect of library work in almost all large libraries. "Acquisitions decisions will be based on extensive management information about collections and users, and ordering and accounting will be done automatically. Cataloguing will be the by-product of shared bibliographic databases. . . . Online user access catalogues and circulation control functions will be commonplace because they have the greatest potential value for users."[7] The user will be able to access both the holdings and current availability status of materials in the entire library system from a terminal in any library location, his office, or perhaps even home. Almost all bibliographic data, as well as a significant percentage of statistical,

scientific, and directory data will be accessed through computer terminals. Given these service conditions, librarians will have to be skillful in both the printed and electronic media if they are to provide an effective service.[8]

Many would agree with Lancaster[9] that paper will not be as important in the information systems of the year 2000 as it is today. There would simply be too much paper, and retrieval of information would be too cumbersome. However, it is unlikely that computer technology will lead to the demise of the library in the foreseeable future. Sales of personal computers are flourishing, but a "computer in every home" is still far from a reality. Similarly, although basic computer literacy is on the rise, relatively few people will have the skills needed for sophisticated information retrieval. Libraries and librarians will not be discarded so easily. New technology is not necessarily desirable just because it is innovative. As O'Connor[10] rather humorously states:

> Twenty years ago the output of a retrieval service consisted of references, perhaps accompanied by abstracts. Since then there have been three revolutions in retrieval hardware: computers, online retrieval, and telecommunications networks. In addition there have been several revolutionary changes in retrieval "software," such as text searching and thesauri. Now, after all these advances, the output of a retrieval service consists of references, possibly accompanied by abstracts.

What one must consider of course is the speed with which the information is obtained. The use of technology is the only way ultimately to manage large, diversified library collections and the overwhelming proliferation of published information. Sack[11] however, on considering whether libraries will disappear in time, suggests that "the library is a modest hurdle to the scholar, with immodest potential. It is hard to use, distant, rule-bound, inflexible, and not readily assimilated to the scholar's work-space and -time." As the library becomes more flexible and service-oriented, however, it actually starts to shape itself to the user, becoming less a specific place than a service, less a collection of books than a means, via the new technologies, to fast and efficient information access and delivery. Sack goes on to suggest that electronic access will require a shift in librarians' service outlook from "owning, cataloguing and lending to becoming electronic data sleuths ready to link a student or faculty member to someone else's data bank." Given that libraries will remain for the foreseeable future, a new look at their approach, functions, and environment is necessary. Rather than being an end in themselves, they are now merely a part of any researcher's information network, the medium via which information is accessed and acquired.

The impact of automation on the physical organization of space and facilities within the library is important. New technology has already had an effect on concept and design, the use of space, the physical environment, and building costs, and these developments and challenges will continue to determine the planning of libraries in the future. The fully electronic library will have sophisticated air conditioning and power requirements, electrical flexibility, and extensive ductwork. It will provide reader stations able to accommodate a wide variety of hardware, and storage systems for a diverse collection of software. It will be conceived as a learning and information center rather than a collection of bookshelves and study spaces.

Any aspect of technology applied to library activities must be designed and introduced so that it will be acceptable to those who will use it. If not, there will be user resistance to both the machine and the system. In staff situations productivity will fall, and in user situations the library will be avoided if possible. The new technology can be restrictive as users are obliged to stay in one place. Physical stress may result from looking at terminal screens for long periods, and adaptation to change may be psychologically stressful. Thus it becomes even more essential that library buildings be designed and furnished with the needs of the user in mind.[12] The challenge to planners and architects will be to ensure that space, color, and visual beauty exist in these electronic spaces.

The increasing need for individual study space is becoming apparent to those concerned with planning the automated library of the present and future.[13] Space norms for study stations will have to allow for more space than in the traditional library. A larger area per reader on an individual basis, either at carrels or tables equipped with electronic or audiovisual devices, will be required to achieve the same overall capacity as the four-, six-, and eight-place tables did in the past. Difficulties could arise if the standards determining study space in academic libraries (approximately 2.5 m^2 or 27 ft^2 per station at present) do not keep pace with developments. To counteract this, it is likely that libraries in the future will be forced to favor reader space over materials space, with the relegation of lesser-used stock to store.

The final appearance of the library, both inside and out, and the way in which it functions, are of concern to both librarian and architect. University libraries are structures that for many decades will remain an example of the architects' work, and they should be encouraged to create a captivating design. In an age where architectural symbolism is outdated and economic strictures place great inhibitions on their work, they deserve sympathetic treatment.[14] The building must survive the developments of the future, providing a functional and efficient physical environment. The full cooperation, support, and imagination of everyone involved in the planning process is essential if the building is to be a success.

REFERENCES

1. N. Lushington, "Some random notes on functional design," *American Libraries*, February 1976, p.92.
2. D. Kaser, "Twenty-five years of academic library building planning," *College and Research Libraries*, July, 1984, p.280.
3. R.H. Rohlf, "Library design: what not to do," *American Libraries*, February 1986, p.100.
4. S.J. Teague, "British university libraries today," *New Library World*, vol.79, no.931, 1978, p.37.
5. R.E. Ellsworth, *Planning Manual for Academic Library Buildings* (Metuchen, N.J.: Scarecrow Press, 1973), p.77.
6. J. Orne, "Library building trends and their meanings," *Library Journal*, December 1977, p.2399.
7. R.W. Boss, *The Library Manager's Guide to Automation*, 2nd ed. (New York: Knowledge Industry Publications, 1984), pp.133–34.
8. Ibid.

9. F.W. Lancaster, *Towards Paperless Information Systems* (New York: Academic Press, 1978), p.1.

10. J. O'Connor (quoted by A.C. Foskett), *Australian Academic and Research Libraries,* vol.13, no.1, 1982, p.46.

11. J.R. Sack, "Open systems for open minds," *College and Research Libraries,* vol.47, no.6, 1986, pp.536–37.

12. Educational Facilities Laboratories, *The Impact of Technology on the Library Building* (New York: E.F.L., 1967), p.20.

13. R.H. Rohlf, "Building-planning implications of automation," *Library Automation: A State of the Art Review.* Papers presented at the Preconference Institute on Library Automation, Information Science and Automation Division of the American Library Association, San Francisco, 1969 (Chicago: ALA, 1969), p.34.

14. J.M. Orr, *Designing Library Buildings for Activity* (London: Andre Deutsch, 1972), p.75.

Index